the Institute *of* Public Relations

PR IN PRACTICE SERIES

EFFECTIVE MEDIA RELATIONS

How to Get Results

Michael Bland, Alison Theaker
& David Wragg

IPR

the Institute *of* Public Relations

**KOGAN
PAGE**

First published in 1996.

Kogan Page Limited
120 Pentonville Road
London N1 9JN

© Michael Bland, Alison Theaker and David Wragg

British Library Cataloguing in Publication Data
A CIP record for this book is available from the British Library.

ISBN 0 7494 1856 7

Typeset by BookEns Ltd, Royston, Herts.
Printed and bound in Great Britain by Biddles Ltd, Guildford and Kings Lynn

Contents

PR in Practice Series

Published in association with the Institute of Public Relations
Consultant Editor: Anne Gregory

Kogan Page has joined forces with the Institute of Public Relations to publish this unique new series which is designed specifically to meet the needs of the increasing numbers of people seeking to enter the public relations profession and the large band of existing PR professionals.

Taking a practical, action-oriented approach, the books in the series will concentrate on the day-to-day issues of public relations practice and management rather than academic theory.

They will provide ideal primers for all those on IPR, CAM and CIM courses or those taking NVQs in PR. For PR practitioners, they will provide useful refreshers and ensure that their knowledge and skills are kept up-to-date.

Anne Gregory is head of the School of Business Strategy and an assistant dean of the Faculty of Business at Leeds Metropolitan University. As former chair of the Institute of Public Relations' Education and Training Committee, Anne initiated the PR in Practice series.

Other titles in the series are:
Planning and Managing a Public Relations Campaign
Anne Gregory
Public Relations in Practice
Edited by Anne Gregory
Forthcoming titles in the series are:
A Practitioner's Guide to Implementing Public Relations
Philip Henslowe
Running a Public Relations Consultancy
Peter Hehir
Running a Public Relations Department
Mike Beard
Strategic Public Relations
Edited by Anne Gregory

Available from all good bookshops, or to obtain further information please contact the publishers at the address below:

Kogan Page Ltd
120 Pentonville Road
London N1 9JN
Tel: 0171 278 0433
Fax: 0171 837 6348

About the authors

Michael Bland worked in Germany, Austria and Switzerland as a sales manager for Reuters Limited. After five years in finance and financial journalism he set up and ran the first PR activity for the Institute of Directors and played a key role in putting it on the map. He then spent six years as head of government relations and corporate public affairs for Ford Motor Company Limited before becoming an independent consultant in 1984. Michael is corporate communications consultant to a number of leading companies and organisations and has trained many hundreds of executives in the techniques of public relations, personal presentation, media interviews and crisis management.

Alison Theaker, MIPR, MA has worked in public relations for eight years, in a variety of in-house positions, including: Performing Right Society, Association of Photographers, Institute of Housing, National Museum of Photography, Film and Television in Bradford, Metropolitan Borough of Rochdale. Specialises in media relations, internal communications, publications. She was the first member of staff appointed to teach on the new BA Hons in Public Relations at the then Leeds Polytechnic (now Leeds Metropolitan University) in 1990. She is a course representative in CERP Education, and delivered a paper to the November 1994 CERP Education Research committee in Brussels on women in PR.

David Wragg is an independent consultant, living and working in Edinburgh. He is the author of 17 books, including 6 on public relations. Formerly Head of Corporate Communications for the Royal Bank of Scotland, his experience in public relations has extended to transport, travel and manufacturing industry, as well as financial services. Before entering public relations, he was a journalist, contributing regularly to *The Sunday Telegraph* and *The Spectator*.

Foreword

To the uninformed, public relations is synonymous with press relations and, indeed, many public relations practitioners spend much of their time dealing with the press. Some spend none of their time on media relations. The stories that journalists relate of the naive practitioner sending the wrong material to the wrong people are legion. They also frequently, and rightly, complain that press material is badly presented as advertising in disguise and of no interest at all to them or their readers. The experts writing here give a practical insight and guide for those wanting to work with journalists.

In Part One, Alison Theaker deals with the media context. Knowing what the rules are as far as slander and libel are concerned, knowing the history of the media and knowing about the shape of things to come is very important. It gives practitioners an understanding of why things are as they are and the constraints that journalists work under.

David Wragg then looks at the written press. He outlines the opportunities that are available and gives practical hints and tips on how to work with them.

Rounding off the book, Michael Bland takes a behind-the-scenes look at radio and television interviews. He gives an insight into how these media work and then lays down easy-to-follow guidelines on how to get the most from the interview, while also giving the journalists what they want.

By reading this book, the newcomer to public relations practice will have a very solid basis on which to work, will be able to provide a professional service to the press and will gain the satisfaction of knowing they have done their job well.

Anne Gregory
Series Editor
IPR/Kogan Page

Introduction

For many public relations practitioners much of their time is taken up with media relations. This book aims to inform them about some of the aspects of the media's development which affect their operation today, as well as offering some practical guidelines on how to work with the media successfully.

The media is central to public relations activity for two reasons: the origins of the industry itself in the press agency of such luminaries as Barnum (who coined the phrase 'There's no such thing as bad publicity') and Ivy Leadbetter Lee (who sent the first press release); and the use of the media in the propaganda campaigns during the two world wars in which British public relations was born.

As well as being a powerful tool to persuade, the media can be used to inform relevant sections of the public. With the use of trade and specialist publications as well as the new broadcast media, the public can be targeted narrowly and effectively. The media can be used to encourage two-way communication, as recently seen in the campaign by Daewoo which encouraged people to respond to their corporate advertising with any complaints about their experiences of buying cars.

Moreover, editorial coverage carries an implicit endorsement of information and is consequently held to be more believable than advertising, which is paid-for and expected to be biased.

By using media relations effectively, public relations practitioners will not only enhance the reputation of their clients or employers, but also themselves, and establish good working relationships with journalists that will serve them well in the future.

PART 1

THE MEDIA CONTEXT

Alison Theaker

1

Where and when: a brief media history

In democratic countries the media likes to regard itself as independent and operating in the interests of the general public. The code of conduct of the National Union of Journalists (NUJ) in the UK states that 'A journalist shall at all times defend the principle of the freedom of the press ... He/she shall strive to eliminate distortion, news suppression and censorship'.

However, in the nineteenth century, the press depended on prior intelligence from government of news stories. This information was conditional upon support for that government. There was no investigative journalism. Libel law was used to control content; stamp duty and various taxes attempted to restrict ownership of the press to 'those who would conduct themselves in a responsible manner' (Cresset Pelham, MP), who were, according to Lord Castlereagh, 'men of respectability and property'. Although in 1836, the London readership of the radical press was 2 million (more than that of the legitimate press) by 1837 these papers had disappeared.

The initial capital to start a paper was small. The Leeds-based *Northern Star* was set up in 1837 at a cost of £690, using a hand press and hired type. By 1839 it was making a profit of £13,000, and the break-even circulation was only 6,200. As the industrial revolution progressed, printing became more mechanised and so more copies could be produced. But mechanisation also increased set-up costs and break-even circulations considerably: in 1896, the *Daily Mail* cost £15,000 to start and in 1918, the *Express* cost £2 million, with a break-even circulation of 250,000.

As the costs and break-even circulations rose, the role of advertising increased. In order to cover costs, newspapers began to aim at the mass market. Working-class papers had large circulations, but little or no advertising. Thus an increase in readership only meant an increase in losses. When the *Daily Herald* was forced to close, it had a circulation of 4.7 million, more than *The Times*, the *Financial Times* and *The Guardian* together. It closed not because people did not want to read it, but because it did not gain enough advertising. Advertisers put their money behind more middle-of-the-road, conservative papers in order to reach the middle and upper classes who had more disposable income. The majority of the press today still support conservative values.

Where: origins of the press in Europe

In France, the newspaper industry grew up against the background of the Press Law in 1881, which declared 'the press is free'. Newspapers were regarded as important both for democracy and for entertainment. Before 1870, the *Petit Journal* had a circulation of 300,000, and on the eve of the First World War there were 60 daily papers in Paris and 250 in the provinces. Many papers sprang from political and religious causes. Since the two world wars the number of titles has declined and circulation has stagnated since the 1940s.

Three kinds of press grew up in Germany. First, a party-related press emerged after the 1848 revolution, integral in the building up of political parties. Secondly, local papers developed in the provinces which carried both non-political editorial and advertising. Thirdly, the boulevard paper was based in large towns and contained sensationalised stories. One hugh press empire emerged in the 1930s under Alfred Hugenberg, whose anti-democratic stance contributed to the downfall of the Weimar Republic. The Nazis took over the German media when they came to power; consequently after the war the Allies created a new press. The British and French set up papers based on a single-party group, while the Americans granted licences to groups representative of a spectrum of opinion.

Where: broadcasting in Europe

UK

In 1922, the British Broadcasting Company began operations, receiving a Royal Charter in 1926 to become the British Broadcasting Corporation. Its stated mission was to inform, educate and entertain.

The BBC gained a national audience in 1926 with the General Strike. Managing Director John Reith stated that, 'the government is acting for the people, so the BBC is for the government'. Statements from strikers and strike-breakers were broadcast, but no representative of organised labour, nor the Leader of the Opposition, Ramsay MacDonald, was allowed to broadcast.

Television broadcasts began in 1936 from Alexandra Palace. Commercial television did not start until 1955, and competition for viewers sectionalised the audience. Although the commercial channel initially struggled to attract viewers, by 1957 Sir Kenneth Clark declared that preference in favour of the new service was 79:21.

France

The broadcast media in France is much more state-controlled than in the UK. Radio broadcasts began in France in 1921, and in 1923 the French state created a monopoly. Permits were sold to private companies for periods of ten years. Radio was dependent on the government to survive, because, even if the channel were a private one, there would be little or no advertising revenue. France was slow to follow Britain in the adoption of television. There were only 300 TV sets in France in 1939, as against 25,000 in Britain. Complete coverage of the country was not achieved until 1961. The state channel RTF was hampered by frequent strikes, and did not broadcast at weekends. The Director-General of the service was a senior civil servant, and the coverage of demonstrations, particularly about Algeria in 1956, was suppressed. Gerard, the head of radio and TV news in 1961, stated 'A journalist should be French first, objective second'. In 1964, the channel became ORTF, and has included serials, thrillers, comedy and games since the early 1970s. However, in 1975 President Giscard d'Estaing promised no government intervention and, since then, relations between government and television have eased.

Germany

In West Germany, Article 5 of the Basic Law passed in 1945 states that 'freedom of the press and freedom of reporting by radio and film is guaranteed'. Nine regional broadcasting stations were set up, four funded by the US and one by the French. As the system was devised after the war, there was a resistance to any kind of centralism or uniformity. Broadcasting was and still is therefore controlled by the regional government rather than being a federal responsibility. The first TV channel is shared by the nine regional companies, and shows regional programmes in the early evening. Finance is provided through licence fees. ZDF, set up in 1961 to give an objective overall view of world events, also supplements its income from advertising. There are two radio stations, DW and DLF. In addition there are six regional radio stations.

2

Who: ownership of the media

Since the Second World War, ownership of the media in the UK has become more concentrated. The share of the three leading corporations, News International, Mirror Group and United Newspapers, rose to 74 per cent of daily-paper circulation in 1993.

Ownership of the media carries with it the possibility to influence editorial content, and this has varied with individual proprietors. This chapter includes a brief overview of the main players in the media world.

Personalities and papers

In the US, William Randolph Hearst, immortalised by Orson Welles' portrayal in *Citizen Kane*, epitomised the model of the newspaper proprietor. In 1887 he took over the *San Francisco Examiner*, and over the following 25 years used the paper to make and break political reputations. Hearst himself almost managed to obtain the Democratic presidential nomination in 1904. This link between political ambitions and influencing opinion through media ownership is a common one.

In the nineteenth century, proprietors tended to run newspapers for non-commercial reasons. Cobbett's *Political Register* lost millions, and George Newnes lost about £10,000 per year with the *Westminster Press*. Newspaper ownership tended to be concentrated in a few families. Alfred Harmsworth (later Lord Northcliffe) fought as a Unionist candidate in Portsmouth in 1895, but, despite the fact that he had bought a local paper to support him, failed to gain a seat. In 1896 he set up the *Daily Mail*, and in 1903 the *Daily Mirror*. He later sold the *Daily Mirror* to his brother Harold (later Lord Rothermere) in 1914. In 1908 Northcliffe had also bought *The Times* from Colonel Astor, whose brother William Waldort Astor bought the *Observer* from Northcliffe in 1911. The final member of this group of press barons was Max Aitken, later Lord Beaverbrook. A Canadian who was MP for Ashton-under-Lyme, Aitken bought the *Daily Express* in order to support Lloyd George against Asquith. He also bought the *Evening Standard* and the *Sunday Express* in 1918.

The *Daily Herald* was the only paper set up as a supporter of the organised labour movement. Begun in 1911 as a strike paper, the TUC owned 49 per cent of the shares. Under editor Julias Elias, later Lord Southwood, circulation rose to 2 million. Due to a shortfall in advertising, this meant the paper lost £3 million per year as more copies meant greater losses. However, other papers were forced to follow suit to keep up in the circulation war.

Many newspapers were run like family businesses, with Cecil Harmsworth King, nephew of the founder, taking over the *Daily Mirror*, and Beaverbrook's son Max Aitken at the *Express*. Roy Thomson, another Canadian, bought *The Times*, although he was forced to sell it in 1969 to another newcomer, Australian Rupert Murdoch. Murdoch had also bought the *Daily Herald*, which had been relaunched as *The Sun* in 1964 by King and failed. Murdoch relaunched the paper again, this time with its familiar brash tabloid style, and circulation rose dramatically. Canadian Conrad Black took over *The Daily Telegraph* in 1985, and Czech-born ex-Labour MP Robert Maxwell took over the *Daily Mirror* in 1984.

The demise of Fleet Street

Many restrictive and protective practices had been enforced by the print unions such as extra payments for work not done, and agreed high manning levels filled by 'ghosts', with surplus wages split between those actually working with shift. Power to negotiate had been devolved to individual 'chapels', and proprietors would often make concessions to union demands in order to get the papers produced. Fleet Street losses totalled £21 million in 1975–6.

In the US, many papers tended to have local monopolies such as the *Los Angeles Times* which attracted 95 per cent of local newspaper advertising. Owners had no fears about suspending circulation in order to achieve the introduction of new technology to reduce costs. Photocomposition, computerised typesetting and web offset printing were introduced. Unlike the UK, the majority of sales were through subscription, rather than street sales. Thus papers adapted the new technology to the needs of their market with zoned editions and special supplements.

Following this example, the introduction of new technology began in 1986 with Eddy Shah's *Today*. Between 1986 and 1989 the power of the print unions was broken, mainly through Rupert Murdoch's movement of his production facilities to Wapping. Other papers followed suit, moving to cheaper sites and selling their Fleet Street premises. Computer typesetting, often direct by the journalist to the page, meant greater efficiency but also higher start-up costs and break-even circulations. Although the *News on Sunday*, *Sunday Correspondent* and *London Daily News* invested £6 million, £18 million and £30 million respectively, all failed because of insufficient capital. Only the *Independent* emerged from this period as a successful new title, and this has recently run into financial difficulties resulting in a large stake being sold to Mirror Group Newspapers.

Ownership in France and Germany

Freedom and diversity are enshrined in the French constitution. Between 1945 and 1974, the number of titles declined sharply, from 175 to 75 regional dailies and 31 to 10 Paris papers; and in the 1970s Robert Hersant emerged as a media baron, with ownership of 16 per cent of the total volume of sales. This was a new development in France and caused something of a political panic. However, the press in France enjoys a number of subsidies, and the state directly and indirectly supports a diversity of publications.

In Germany, there is a similar fear of media concentration. Although there are over 1,200 regional newspapers in Germany, they form 122 'editorial unities' through arrangements of co-ownership and co-operation and one-quarter of the population lives in an area of virtual newspaper monopoly. The most important chain is Springer, which controls 25 per cent of the total circulation.

Cross-media ownership

Associated Newspapers owns the *Daily Mail*, the *Mail on Sunday* and numerous regional papers and also has interests in Westcountry TV, Classic FM and Great Western Radio in the UK, as well as connections with Herald-Sun TV in Australia and Harmsworth House publications in the US. EMAP owns 70 regional newspapers, 156 consumer and business magazines and has interests in a number of local radio stations. News International owns newspapers in the UK (*Times, Sun, News of the World, Sunday Times*), US (*Boston Herald, New York Post*), Australia (*The Australian*), and the Far East. As well as magazine publishing and film and television interests across the world, one of Murdoch's more controversial holdings is his 50 per cent stake in BSkyB. He was exempted from the provisions of the 1990 Broadcasting Act so that he could own both newspapers and a substantial part of the monopoly satellite broadcasting company.

The 1995 Green Paper recommended that newspaper groups with less than 20 per cent of national circulation should be allowed to own terrestrial TV stations, exceeding 15 per cent of the television market. Thus groups like Pearson, Associated Newspapers, the *Guardian* and the *Telegraph*, which formed the lobbying organisation British Media Industry Group, would be able to extend their interests into television.

Cross-media ownership is regulated in the US by the Federal Communications Commission (FCC). The ownership of a TV station and daily newspaper in the same area is prohibited, in the interests of diversity of viewpoint.

In June 1995, the Italian electorate voted in a referendum to let right-wing leader Silvio Berlusconi keep his three TV channels. They also indicated that they were favourable to the privatisation of the state-owned broadcasting system, RAI.

What now?

Increasing costs can only lead to a concentration of ownership, as only the larger players will be able to set up and run the new forms of the media. As fewer players are left on the media stage, editorial policies will tend to follow a less radical line. This will increase the effort necessary to obtain coverage by the larger groups, and will also increase the importance of smaller, specialised titles for public relations practitioners.

3

Media law

Contempt of court

The media may run the risk of breaking the Contempt of Court Act if they comment on active proceedings, jury deliberations, criticise the judiciary or disobey a court order. Any writing, speech or broadcast may be treated as contempt, regardless of intent, but the relevant piece must create a substantial risk of serious impediment or prejudice to particular legal proceedings. Prejudicial media coverage has recently led to the abandonment of several prosecutions. However, the Act also states that publication may not be contempt if part of such a discussion is 'in good faith'. This originally related to an article which the *Sunday Times* wished to publish in 1974 about thalidomide, when civil proceedings were pending on behalf of several children who had been affected by the drug.

Libel and slander

A statement which tends to lower a person in the estimation of 'right-thinking members of society' or which may injure that person in their office, profession or trade, is defamation. The two main types are: libel, if the statement is made in a permanent form, such as writing, radio or television; and slander, if the statement is transitory, like speech. Every publication constitutes a fresh offence, so that any libel appearing in a newspaper could result in actions against the writer, editor, printer, publisher and distributor.

Jurors have to decide whether the words used were in fact defamatory, in the circumstances. Of course words mean different things to different people. Another problem is changing standards: for instance, a court ruled during the First World War that it was libel to write of someone that he was a German.

Public relations practitioners should bear this in mind when issuing statements to the media, especially those involving competitors. It may also be counter-productive to take legal action in some cases, as McDonald's have discovered to their cost in prosecuting two demonstrators for making statements about their practices. The resulting media coverage has done more damage than the original statements.

Codes of conduct

As well as the law, there are also various codes of conduct which apply to the media. The NUJ *Code of Conduct* states that 'A journalist has a duty to maintain the highest professional and ethical standards'. Those who have had experience of tabloid methods may not feel that this code has much effect. Other elements of the code exhort the journalist to strive to eliminate distortion and news suppression, to make sure that information is accurate, to correct any harmful inaccuracies and protect confidential sources of information. Photographs should only be obtained by straightforward means, and not intrude into grief or distress unless it is in the public interest. Journalists are not to take advantage of confidential information before it is made public, nor to distort the truth because of advertising considerations or endorse any commercial product. Mentioning race, colour, creed, illegitimacy, disability, marital status, gender or sexual orientation should only be included where strictly relevant to the story. These considerations should be borne in mind by the public relations practitioner.

The Press Complaints Commission (PCC) is a body set up by the media to regulate its own affairs. The PCC provides an opportunity for injured parties to reply to news coverage. Payment for stories is not permitted, except where the story is in the public interest and payment is necessary for this to happen.

However, these codes are as yet only voluntary, and any complaint over inaccurate coverage may raise more problems.

Broadcasting codes

If there is misrepresentation on television, there are two routes for complaints. The Broadcasting Standards Council deals with sex, violence, taste and decency. Complaints can be made about the content of radio and television programmes and advertise-ments, and must be made within two months of the broadcast. The other body is the Broadcasting Complaints Commission (BCC), which deals with unfair treatment or infringement of privacy in television or radio programmes or advertisements, including satellite and cable as well as terrestrial channels. Organisations or individuals may complain, and the BCC may consider a complaint on behalf of someone who has died providing the programme was made within five years of their death.

Investigations may take several weeks, and adjudications are normally broadcast at a similar time to the programme which was the subject of the complaint.

Time for a change?

There are a variety of approaches to media reform. The

Campaign for Press and Broadcasting Freedom is concerned about the concentration of the media in the hands of fewer and larger conglomerates (see chapter 2) as well as restrictions on reporting. They propose a Freedom of Information Act on the US model, allowing access to government papers; repealing the Contempt of Court and Official Secrets Acts; and replacing the PCC with an independent body which would enforce a general right to reply to inaccurate reporting and monitor press standards.

At the time of writing, there is no clear indication of how the debate may be resolved.

4

Ethics and privacy

While television is regarded as the most important source of news in Britain, the press is generally held in low esteem. This is especially the case with the tabloid papers. The 1990 Calcutt Committee made some attempts to address the questions of privacy and honesty. The Government is reluctant to introduce legislation which could be seen as gagging the free press. While reporting is an interpretation of the facts, which involves selection and ordering of the text, there is continuing concern about some of the more sensationalist writing in the tabloids.

The Independent Broadcasting Authority (IBA) Act of 1973 specifically refers to 'due impartiality' in cases of 'political or industrial controversy relating to current public policy'. Impartiality is also enshrined in the BBC's Charter. However, reports of the activities of royalty and politicians in the press over the past years were instrumental in leading to the Calcutt Committee's proposals (see below). The involvement of publicists in the promotion of some obviously untrue stories has reflected poorly on public relations as a profession. For the most case, the publicist is not distinguished in the public's mind from the public relations professional. Cases such as the sale of photographs of the Princess of Wales, taken without her knowledge, to a national tabloid and the invention of affairs between ex-politicians and actresses, have caused the reputation of the media to sink even lower.

In Germany, pressure on broadcasters led to the so-called Statutes Movement. Pressure to conform to party-political ideas led Wolf Donner to say: 'It is less a question of concrete cases than of an atmosphere, of an indirect, difficult to prove, anonymous censorship.' Reaction to this movement tended to focus on a perceived (but not demanded) right of journalists to have more say in the content of programmes which they produce. Eventually a much-weakened version of the journalists' demands was introduced, which introduced some guarantees of the rights of the individual broadcaster more in keeping with the Basic Law.

In France, radio news has been generally recognised as more impartial than television news, although more people have come to rely on television as their major source of information, as in Britain. Television news has been strictly controlled, with the fair allocation of broadcasting time controlled by an independent commission.

In the US, there is a significant difference in the behaviour of the media. Discussions are aired regularly about ethics in the media. The different operational framework may be one of the reasons. Because the majority of papers are city or region based rather than national, they are interested in maintaining a relationship with their readers. Also, because of the larger number of graduate journalism courses, journalism has a more academic foundation than in Britain. Richard Harwood, ombudsman of the *Washington Post* deals with complaints about how the paper deals with stories, and writes a regular column with the results of his investigations. Journalists rely on the First Amendment: 'Congress shall make no law ... abridging the freedom of speech or of the press.'

The Hutchins Commission reported in 1947 and criticised the media for 'meaningless, flatness, distortion and the perpetuation of misunderstanding'. Newspapers have a more serious attitude to corrections, with two-thirds being made within two days of the original error. Apparently the *Boston Globe* once apologised because 'statements made by Sylvester the Cat were erroneously attributed to Daffy Duck'. After the failure of the National News Council in 1973, there have been calls for the media to carry out ethical audits to check the accuracy of their stories. However, more recently there has been concern about the outbreak of 'sleaze' journalism, and the conflicting treatment given to stories in the press and on television. The coverage of the OJ Simpson trial is a good example of a sensational story which has been rendered banal by over-exposure. The exhaustive, direct coverage of the court proceedings would be impossible in Britain.

Regulation

Concerns about press standards have led to discussions about regulation of the media. One of the main concerns has been privacy of the individual, and what constitutes a news story or a gratuitous invasion into someone's private life. In 1989, two Private Member's Bills put forward were concerned with press excesses, a Right of Reply Bill by Tony Worthington and a Privacy Bill by John Browne. Neither Bill succeeded, but pressure for action caused the Calcutt Committee to be set up. This looked at privacy and the press and published its report in 1990. In an attempt to counteract any extreme recommendations, national newspapers appointed ombudsmen to deal with readers' complaints. However, the fact that they were employed by the paper which they were investigating cast doubts on their impartiality. While the committee was preparing its final report, journalists from the *Sunday Sport* infiltrated a hospital ward and interviewed a seriously ill actor, Gordon Kaye, and took pictures of him in his hospital bed. The report and pictures were eventually published, even though Kaye was so ill that he could not recall the interview having taken place. The Court of Appeal lifted an injunction on publication on condition that the paper made it plain that the story had been obtained without consent.

The seven-strong Committee led by David Calcutt QC comprised two lawyers, a journalist, a businesswoman, a professor and an MP. It was unable to prove in any way that standards in the press had significantly declined during this century. However, both the public and parliament had a perception that behaviour had worsened. Representations from individuals were heard, as well as from Robert Maxwell, Rupert Murdoch and Kelvin MacKenzie, editor of *The Sun*. The Committee was considering a non-legislative adjudicating body for the press, when the *Sunday Sport* affair occurred. What resulted was that the final recommendations of the Committee did include a last chance for self-regulation, abolishing the Press Council and replacing it with the Press Complaints Commission, but with the proviso that if this did not improve the situation within 18 months then a statutory tribunal should be set up, presided over by a judge. Three new criminal offences were put forward, that could be committed only by journalists: physical intrusion into people's homes; taking photographs by telephoto lens without permission; and trespass. Two possible events were to trigger the introduction of statutory control: the failure of the media to set up the Press Complaints Commission within 12 months; or non-compliance with Commission's adjudications.

The Press Complaints Commission was set up in January 1991, headed by Lord McGregor, and in the first six months of its existence adjudicated on cases involving Clare Short MP and the *News of the World*, and the *Daily Star* for an article headlined 'Poofters on Parade' about recommendations of a Select Committee that homosexuals should be allowed to serve in the armed forces. However, calls for more controls on press and broadcasters often came from politicians who felt they had been unfairly interrogated, such as Jonathan Aitken MP who protested about his treatment by John Humphreys of the BBC's *Today* programme.

The Government has not acted on the tougher recommendations of the Committee, and the case for or against regulation has not been resolved. In broadcasting, the BBC suffers from the fact that the Government regards it as anti-Conservative, despite its being called both the Baghdad Broadcasting Corporation and the Blair Broadcasting Corporation by MPs offended by particular coverage. The Glasgow Media Unit would argue that both BBC and ITV are pro-establishment.

The publishing of information relating to the activities of some MPs led to recommendations by the Nolan Committee in 1995 that MPs should not be paid for consultancy work. The debate over the declaration of interests goes on, affecting the relationship between MPs and public affairs consultancies and lobbyists.

5

Broadcasting in the UK

In 1990, the Broadcasting Act set out the conditions under which TV was to operate for the near future. As well as details of how the next round of ITV franchises, to run from 1 January 1993, would be awarded, it confirmed the BBC as the cornerstone of broadcasting in the UK and ensured that both ITV and BBC would commission 25 per cent of their output from independent production companies.

The franchise battle

ITV franchises are initially awarded for ten years, but companies can re-apply after six years for an extension. Franchises were to be awarded to the highest bidder by the Independent Television Commission, but fears that this would lead to mediocrity and lobbying by incumbent franchise holders resulted in a quality threshold being inserted. Bids were submitted in May 1992 and the ITC announced its decision in October. Fifteen regional licenses (two in the London area) were awarded in the fourteen regions, as well as a national breakfast-television licence.

From the beginning there were major criticisms of the bidding system. All media were scathing about it. Michael Kuhn, part of a group challenging LWT, said that the chances of a new company gaining a franchise from an incumbent was 80:20 against. There were ambiguities about who could bid and the Office of Fair Trading looked at changes to the conditions to avoid monopolies. Originally, companies could not bid for neighbouring franchises.

In formulating bids the pattern of TV advertising had to be estimated for the next 10 to 16 years. This required an educated guess about what effect the penetration of cable and satellite, and the launch of Channel 5 during the franchise period would have. Speculation was also rife that with the BBC's Charter up for renewal in 1996, advertising could be allowed on BBC channels.

Mandated hours were set out for news, current affairs, children's and religious programmes. Bidders had to supply evidence of financial stability and technical standards, including details of the facilities they intended to use. Shareholders had to be shown to have commitment and supply credible financial forecasts.

In the resulting decisions, four companies lost their franchises to new challengers. In three areas, Border, Scottish and Central, there were no challengers. Four incumbent companies (Tyne Tees, Anglia, HTV and Yorkshire) retained their franchises by making the highest bid. In Yorkshire's case, their bid was £37 million, as against the nearest competitor with £17 million. Five companies, Channel Islands, LWT, Grampian, Ulster and Granada, retained their franchises despite making lower bids. The ITC based its decisions on whether the applicants would be able to 'maintain [their] proposed service throughout the period for which the licence would be in force'.

Thames and TV-AM lost their franchises to Carlton and Sunrise respectively, who both bid substantially more, but TVS and TSW lost theirs because they bid substantially higher than Meridian and Westcountry TV and were judged to be unrealistic in claiming to be able to maintain this revenue.

PR in the franchise battle

The approaches of a successful incumbent, YTV, and a successful challenger, Meridian, can be compared. YTV linked increased efficiency with an energetic lobbying campaign. Overtime was cut from £9 million to £2 million, and 33 per cent of staff were made redundant. Lobbying was carried out at Westminster and Whitehall stressing the quality of YTV programmes. ITC members were approached to impress them that YTV was a regional company, linked to local charities and running seven regional offices. Local beneficiaries of donations were asked to write to the chair of the ITC, George Russell, to back this up, as well as commercial, industrial and artistic organisations in the region. Poster advertising campaigns were undertaken both in the region and nationally, emphasising the quality of news, drama and comedy produced by YTV. A press campaign promoted YTV programmes and, by a stroke of luck, one of them, *The Darling Buds of May*, obtained the best network slot during the period of the ITC deliberations and gained top ratings. YTV also conducted an intelligence-gathering exercise to find out about competitors and to assess their strengths.

Meridian used a more private strategy, beginning with a campaign for quality TV, and lobbying for the inclusion of the quality threshold. Meridian set up a network of regional PR consultancies to work for them and did not declare the area they were to bid for until two weeks before the deadline. Interest and awareness in the press was raised, and was used in approaching local opinion formers. Favourable press coverage included an article suggesting that most media correspondents considered Meridian to be the most impressive challenger, and that TVS was the incumbent most likely to lose.

Future of ITV

All incumbents were producer-broadcasters, with their own in-house staff to make programmes. All challengers were publisher-broadcasters, relying on a much smaller core staff, commissioning their programmes from the independent sector. For example, Thames had 1,200 staff as opposed to Carlton's 400. They did not intend to commission in the Channel 4 model, which tends to contract out many one-off programmes, but build up long-term relationships with production houses, commissioning regular series.

The market element of the process emphasised the need for broadcasters to make money. Paul Jackson of Carlton TV said: 'The function of the ITV system is to make programmes people want to watch and get the revenue that comes from it.'

In November 1993, the government relaxed its rules on ownership of franchises, opening the way for a series of mergers to enable ITV companies to compete on a worldwide platform. This is likely to affect programming, and may reduce the regional emphasis of ITV.

The future of PR in ITV

Most contractors' public relations operations have been reduced since the franchises were awarded. All four of YTV's press officers were made redundant and publicity was devolved to programme producers. Contractors are no longer guaranteed slots in the schedule, so publicity and ratings have increased in importance, yet departments are being cut back. Peter Moth, controller of public affairs at Tyne Tees, said: 'In-house departments are coming into their own in all other industries. All the TV companies are cutting back on central services, including PR. That is a serious error.' Despite calls for ITV to be promoted from the centre as a brand, no agreement has been reached by the independent contractors on the method of doing this or how to fund it.

Consequences for the BBC

In order to retain its Charter, the BBC will be expected to prove that it provides value for money, in an environment of increased competition from a greater number of radio and television services. In its 1992 document, *Extending Choice*, the BBC set out its purpose: to provide services of 'an unusually high quality that might be at risk in a purely commercial market'. Its original aims to 'inform, educate and entertain' were still included in the document, as well as impartial journalism, extending the range of drama, supporting improving standards of education and reflecting international development and perspectives. The BBC argued that these objectives were best met by 'a broadcasting organisation which offers programmes of quality across all media', and that this should continue to be funded by the licence fee because 'freedom from the commercial pressures to maximise audience ratings and share' was necessary to produce the proposed range of programmes. Increased accountability was offered through better systems for complaint and redress, and the introduction of performance indicators. Other roles currently performed by the BBC, such as an educator and standard setter in the industry (spending £20 million on training) and a cultural patron (supporting five orchestras and commissioning new works from composers and writers) are likely to be affected by an increased emphasis on cost efficiency.

In 1993, the National Heritage Select Committee report supported the continuance of the licence-fee system, praised the BBC's programme quality and affirmed its role in national life.

In November 1993, a suggestion by the *Financial Times*' deputy editor Ian Hargreaves that the BBC should be privatised brought widespread condemnation in the media world, and repeatedly the dangers of a multi-channel environment like that in the US were quoted as militating against the production of quality programmes. Despite the National Heritage Select Committee report's recommendations, the future of the BBC is far from certain.

6

New media technology

Of course, anything written about new technology at the moment is almost out of date by the time it is printed. Developments in the printed media have been touched on in previous chapters, with the introduction of new printing processes and direct input by journalists which have enabled newspapers to be printed more efficiently and much faster. Heat-set colour instead of photogravure techniques enabled newspapers to produce better colour magazines on ordinary newsprint with a turnaround of four days as opposed to four weeks for a colour supplement on glossy paper. However, the fastest developments are in the broadcast and on-line media, and it is those that will be examined here.

Radio

The main developments in radio in the UK have been the increase of commercial stations, including several nationwide commercial franchises, including Classic FM, Virgin and Talk Radio. Community stations are growing in number. The Integrated Systems Digital Network (ISDN) is a digital telephone line which can transmit broadcast quality audio direct to radio stations, enabling more direct access to programming. Community radio has existed for some time elsewhere in Europe, the US, Canada and Australia, where it has been recognised as providing a local service.

Satellite television

Direct Broadcasting by Satellite (DBS) was first envisaged in 1945 by science-fiction writer Arthur C Clarke, but it was not until 1962 that the first international communications satellite, Telstar, was launched. In 1978, Eutelsat was launched, which was used by the first satellite programmes broadcast from Britain by Satellite TV in 1982 from their studios just off Carnaby Street. Because of legislation they could not be received in this country. They broadcast to Norway and Finland, who had relaxed their broadcasting laws, but at that time there were no policies on such broadcasts agreed across Europe. After a year, Rupert Murdoch bought the ailing company and Sky Television was born. Murdoch himself has referred to the development of satellite broadcasting as 'the most important development since Caxton and the printing press'.

At first, Sky was only available through a cable network system which received the signals and broadcast it through cable to a test area of 10,000 homes in the Swindon area. In 1986 the Independent Broadcasting Authority awarded the franchise for satellite broadcasting in the UK to British Satellite Broadcasting (BSB) but stipulated that a high-quality system be used. Known as MAC, or Multiple Analogue Component system, this was thought to give superior picture quality to the alternative PAL (Phase Alternate Line). BSB had to design and launch its own satellite and was unable to utilise the private Astra satellite, launched in 1988. In 1989, using Astra and PAL, Sky broadcast four channels direct to homes in Britain before BSB had even launched its satellite, and picture quality was found to be adequate after all. The consequent competition between Sky and

BSB for the audience resulted in high financial losses for both companies, which led to their eventual merger in 1990 to form British Sky Broadcasting, or BSkyB. Even so, by the end of 1990, only 10 per cent of British homes had purchased satellite dishes.

BSkyB is in a unique situation in Europe in that it owns the means of distribution, the satellite, and also is a provider of the service, ie Sky Channel. Pay-TV channels, such as Sky Sport and the Movie Channel, are also broadcast this way by using an encoded signal which can only be unscrambled at the user's home by use of a 'smart card'. To receive one of the cards viewers subscribe to the service in addition to the costs of the satellite system.

Channels available tend to be either general entertainment, re-broadcast local services, or specialised or narrowcast services, like CNN (Cable News Network).

International broadcasting is undertaken by Murdoch's Star TV from Singapore, using Asiasat which covers an area from Turkey to Japan. Problems arose in 1989 after pictures of the Tiananmen Square protests and their suppression by the Chinese authorities were broadcast on one of the channels included in the Star package, BBC World Service News. The Chinese government threatened to block Star TV as it could not control the information distributed. In order to keep the lucrative market, Star chose to delete the BBC news from its broadcasts to China. Star TV also broadcasts to India, where local entrepreneurs with satellite dishes took the opportunity to cable their neighbourhoods and set up as small-scale service operators. There are now over 60,000 cable operators in India. India had previously only had a state-controlled monopoly service, Doorshana, which was used basically as a government information channel and was consequently thought to be dull. Star also bought 50 per cent of local station Zee TV in December 1994, a station aimed at the younger end of the market.

Cable television

Cable television originally began as a means to transmit terrestrial television channels to those homes which could not receive broadcasts and developed alongside broadcast TV in the 1950s. Now these systems carry other channels and services. Picture quality was originally poor, but was acceptable on the premise that anything was better than nothing. The Federal Communications Commission began to regulate cable in the US from 1962. Seven towns were selected as pioneers for cable in 1973 in France, including Grenoble, Creteil, Cergy-Pontoise, Nice, Chamonix, Rennes and Metz, and the High Audiovisual Council was created.

In 1981, the British government licensed a small number of pay-TV systems in Britain, but originally no advertising or sponsorship was permitted. In 1984 the Cable Authority was established under the Cable and Broadcasting Act to promote, license and regulate the industry. In Europe, Belgium, the Netherlands and Switzerland are the most highly cabled countries. France is the least cabled.

Essentially, cable broadcasts are received by the cable-provider's antenna, and then re-transmitted through fibre-optic or co-axial cable to the homes of subscribers. Other kinds of data can also be transmitted through cable, and one of the most exiting future developments is set to be the introduction of interactive systems, whereby subscribers can watch programmes and select, for example, a camera angle for an action replay. The development and installation of fibre-optic cables, which provide the opportunity for a greater amount of information to be transmitted, will enable companies in future to have direct connections with consumers in their own homes. This will obviously have implications for public relations practitioners in targeting relevant sections of the public.

Around 1 million consumers subscribe to cable in Britain. Approximately 25 companies have been granted franchises to set up cable systems to cover virtually the whole of the country. British Telecom was not permitted to compete for the cable television service, but new franchisees are permitted to offer an alternative telephone system to their subscribers. In the US, companies cannot operate both telephone and cable television systems. One of the chief advantages for providers of cable systems is that they are able to target areas very directly, with, for example, local news and weather.

The quality of programming on the new variety of channels has been called into question: with so many channels to fill and profits to make, the recycling of old programmes (on channels such as UK Gold) has become commonplace. Other channels, such as CNN, a 24-hour news channel which is also transmitted via satellite, have a high reputation because of their specialist nature. CNN gained much praise from its coverage of the Gulf War, and there was even an instance in 1987 where a remark which President Reagan made about the state of the dollar resulted in the currency coming under attack within 15 minutes of the CNN broadcast. The consequent developments were of course broadcast on CNN within minutes. This illustrates the increased speed of the transmission systems.

To take advantage of the local targeting, Channel One, a cable news service for London, was launched in December 1994. Plans have been made to extend this kind of service to other towns. Channel One is owned by Associated Newspapers, and benefits from cross-promotional activities in the *Daily Mail*. Thirty video-journalists were employed to act as both video-camera operators and journalists, reducing the news teams to one person. However, as there are only 300,000 cable subscribers in London, to date Channel One does not look set to emulate CNN's success as a worldwide 24-hour cable news provider. The latest development in the UK is the launch of Live TV, owned by the Mirror Group and headed by Kelvin MacKenzie, which will supply 24-hour programming.

Internet

This is perhaps the most widely hyped and least understood development in the field of communications. Originally developed in the 1960s by the Pentagon, the Internet is a loosely linked system of various computer networks, joined by modems and telephone lines. The US military withdrew from the system when it became obvious that there was not enough data security on the network. JANET (Joint Academic Network) is one of the networks currently available, which as its name suggests links universities and colleges. Communications can be sent to network users all over the world through the use of an e-mail address. E-mail is the most widely used feature on the Internet. Letters and other communications can be sent directly to another user's computer, where they are stored until read. Media contact is becoming more common via e-mail, and many journalists like to be contacted in this way. A recent survey found that 91 per cent of journalists prefer to receive copy electronically.

Internet users buy a modem connection, and usually subscribe to a local service provider, who charges them for the lease of international telephone lines supplied by BT or AT&T. After subscription, the cost to users is that of the telephone call.

As the telephone system has been updated with fibre-optic cable, so the quality of pictures and graphics which can be sent via the Internet has improved. With ISDN (mentioned above) CD-quality audio and video can also be sent. This may have applications, for example, in the music business, where interested consumers will be able to access video and audio clips of favourite artists' new albums before purchase, as well as detailed information about them. The only limit to this is the time factor involved to download information onto one's own computer, which is extended for graphics, video and music.

The Internet is a vast information source, but there are no directories to enable users to find information which they may be interested in. It depends on users browsing through the various information sources available. The World Wide Web was developed in the 1990s by European scientists. Pages of information on the Web consist of text, graphics and hypertext. The latter enables users to highlight words using a computer mouse, and connect with other linked pages on the Internet.

Neither the Internet nor the World Wide Web are regulated, so it is difficult to know exactly how useful it will be to PR professionals in the future. Lawyer Martha Siegel has warned: 'PR companies that don't get on-line will suffer.' However, companies that transgress 'Netiquette' by sending commercial material to users who do not wish to receive it are liable to be 'flamed', or receive a barrage of hate mail. Siegel, with her partner, Cantor, issued a blanket advertisement for their law practice which resulted in 25,000 flames, which not only crashed their own system but that of the server which linked them to the net and several systems in the surrounding area.

At the moment, the majority of people have no idea of how to get involved with the Internet, nor why they should want to. Although the Internet is more advanced in the US, possibly because of cheaper telephone costs, at any one time the number of people accessing the net there is less than the audience of a TV station in Philadelphia. Most users are male and under 30. Worldwide, there are 30 million users.

However, Two Ten Communications in the UK has already announced a new service to distribute press releases via the Internet. Distributing releases in this way avoids clogging up journalists' fax machines with reams of paper, while targeting worldwide. There is no way to track whether a release has been delivered to the person who has been targeted, or even that the release has been read: some users build in an automatic delete facility for certain kinds of material from certain sources. Releases can also be sent to an incorrectly named e-mail address.

Future developments

Digital TV is likely to be the next development in media technology. Using telephone lines, and compressing electronic information digitally, consumers will gain access to hundreds of television programmes worldwide. New decoders will be required, rendering previous systems obsolete. Media companies are now merging to gear up for this next leap forward: BSkyB, the French Canal, Plus, and Germany's Bertelsmann have formed an alliance to launch digital TV across Europe. It is advisable for PR practitioners to keep a watching brief on the availability of different media tools, while keeping a healthy scepticism.

7

What is it all for? Media evaluation

Evaluation has been growing in importance in professional public relations. Keith Henshall, IPR President in 1995, has stated: 'For PR to be accepted as a management discipline, evaluation is the key.'

Methods of evaluation

Traditionally, there were two schools of thought over measuring the success of any public relations activity. The first believed that the results of good PR were intangible and impossible to measure. The second school of thought consisted of those who looked at the number of press cuttings: if these increased, it was good; if these decreased, it was bad.

A variation on the second school was to measure the volume of cuttings against the cost of advertising in the media. This ignored two significant factors. The first was that some media, notably the BBC in the UK, do not carry advertising. The second was the impact of positive editorial coverage, which is always higher than that of advertising.

Research

Another method which has found favour in recent years is that of research. Before-and-after research can assess the impact of a campaign in terms of the way in which an organisation and its products or activities are viewed by the target audience. This may be extended into regular annual surveys.

Surveys of journalists or investment analysts assess their opinion of an organisation, often expressed in a favourability/familiarity chart. A cost-effective way of doing this is to subscribe to the regular research conducted by MORI into the perceptions which business and financial journalists have of companies. MORI provides important indicators of the way in which specialised journalists view a particular sector.

The MORI research is a good method of assessing not just the views of these important opinion formers of the organisation but most especially it shows how they view the press relations activities of companies. Subscribing to the MORI surveys over a period of time can also track performance of public relations activities.

A specifically commissioned communications audit can focus on those journalists who are known to be of importance to a particular client. It can also be extended so that comparisons are drawn between the company's performance and that of named competitors.

Tracking studies of the corporate image, or regular analyses of audience attitudes, can be helpful in some sensitive fields, such as nuclear energy or pharmaceuticals manufacture. Pre- and post-campaign research is helpful in assessing whether objectives have been attained, but campaigns have to be significant to justify the time, effort and cost of research, which needs to be conducted by an independent and experienced external source.

Media content analysis

Current thought now contends that press coverage has to be

measured and evaluated. Different publications will have a different impact on the audiences, as will the position and the length of any pieces about an organisation. Most important of all is the question of whether the coverage is favourable or unfavourable, or perhaps somewhere between these two extremes.

Some of the various services available to PR practitioners are now reviewed.

CARMA

Set up in 1984, CARMA is one of the few companies which offer international analysis, with offices in the US, Europe, Canada and Australia. CARMA offers initial image assessment, campaign evaluation, competitor benchmarking and journalist analysis. Tracking of issues details emerging and current issues and the likely media response. Trend monitoring will look at a client's media profile over time; media favourability assesses treatment in different media and analyses its importance; and the sources who are quoted as experts can also be pinpointed.

Cutting Edge

This is a software package run on an IBM-compatible system. It is mainly concerned with the UK media. Cuttings have to be analysed, with ratios included for stories, messages, publications and reporters. This requires the client to make a value judgement in assessing these ratios. An analysis for each clipping is then entered into the computer. An advertising-equivalent value is then attached to it, multiplied by the ratios mentioned above.

Media Works

This is part of the Romeike & Curtice group and offers cuttings presentation services as well as analysis. Summary reports are produced at the end of an agreed period. Costs vary according to the amount of information extracted from each cutting, such as equivalent advertising cost, comparison with competitors, bias, key words and messages, company references, links to press releases, spokesperson and size of article. Data can also be stored and comparisons made over time.

Precis

Offered by CMS (Computerised Media Services), this is the only system to be recognised by the Public Relations Consultants Association (PRCA). A value is attached to each piece of media coverage to try and ascertain its impact. This relates to the size of the cutting in relation to the format of the publication, position, presence of a picture, status of publication and attitude of the journalist. Competitive analysis is also available. Cuttings can be held on database for retrieval. Precis covers the UK and Europe and can also be used to track issues in the media. A comparison with advertising effectiveness is possible.

Impacon

Impacon uses its own IMAGING computer system to analyse and present data. Up to 174 different codes can be attached to any one piece of media coverage, from date, source and author to content, attitude and effect, related to the client and their staff. Records can be retrieved according to a variety of criteria, for example all coverage which mentioned the client in an unfavourable way related to a particular message. The statistics option converts this into tables and charts. Information can also be cross-analysed. Sources and authors can be listed according to a variety of criteria, and profiles can be drawn up. Marketing services are available to assess the impact of media coverage on company image and the effect that has on sales, profits and products.

Media Measurement

This company offers two services, Press Relations Performance Review and Strategic Media Monitor. The former was developed in the late 1980s and analyses coverage in terms of its favourability. Media attitudes towards the client are assessed, and over time shifts and trends can be defined. Historical analysis of how individual publications regarded the issues involved can be accessed, and lists of sources used by the media and bylined journalists can be provided. SMM was developed in 1994 to identify, track and evaluate corporate, brand and issue coverage. The statistical model used can produce definitions of the environment, analysis of issues, and hierarchical relationships between characteristics. The client can vary the specification and up to 5000 attributes, or different characteristics, can be included. The effect of issues on a company can be assessed. Opinion polling can be developed through readership analysis. The two systems offer both the effectiveness of media relations and the possibility of predicting and planning for the emergence of issues.

Metrica

This company offers two evaluation systems. CIGMA is a media evaluation system, giving feedback on media coverage. Individual programmes are developed with clients. Analysis of back coverage is available for benchmarking. Media coverage is broken down into context units to reduce the subjective nature of the analysis, and a balance of favourability is obtained. Readership data is obtained from a regularly updated database, and competitor analysis is available. COMM-MAP is a method of evaluation which focuses on non-media-related PR activities. Again, individual 'templates' are developed for each client, linked to relevant goals, messages and audiences. This involves a rolling programme of meetings to assess past activities and to plan for future ones.

Coverage versus content

All the systems available involve at some point an evaluation of the coverage received. However many attributes this process can cope with, a subjective measure of favourability and importance of publication must be made, although the different systems may offer different degrees of subjectivity.

It is also possible to use systems such as FT Profiles from the *Financial Times*, and its Reuters equivalent, to survey an organisation's press coverage. Systems such as FT Profiles do not place a value on media coverage, and do not provide a favourability rating. One advantage of media content analysis, which considers the quality of coverage as well as the quantity, is that it indirectly takes account of stories which would reflect adversely on the organisation had they appeared.

It also recognises the work of the press office in minimising the impact of bad publicity, and can demonstrate the importance of good issues or crisis-management programmes in terms which company managements will be able to recognise.

CARMA claim that public opinion mirrors media coverage and so is one of the best indicators of how companies are perceived. Of course, sometimes life is much simpler.

Small companies with a simple need to generate enquiries may use response rates to assess how worthwhile press relations are to their business.

Even larger organisations can sometimes find that press relations success can be evaluated simply by the impact on business. In one case, a bank using a system of localising press releases to heighten awareness of individual branches had a small four-paragraph news item about a new mortgage product appear in the *Western Morning News*. The product was not being advertised, but within two weeks the branch at Plymouth gained £900,000 of mortgage business.

No system of evaluation is worth paying for unless measurable, specific objectives are first set. This ensures that correct measurement criteria can be agreed. Evaluation must be planned from the start and should be continuous. *Ad hoc* data has only a limited validity and use. Although there is still room for further development, these systems do provide one way of demonstrating results from a major area of PR activity. The planning and objective setting involved can also be useful to the practitioner in focusing effort into cost-effective channels.

PART 2

DEALING WITH THE PRESS

David Wragg

8

What: newspapers and periodicals

While the press has become less important in the eyes of many because of the growth in broadcasting of all kinds, it remains vitally important in reaching many audiences and for many messages. In the UK, there are more than 2,000 newspapers.

Targeting

This wide variety of media provides an opportunity for the public relations practitioner. The wide range of daily and weekly newspapers published outside London enables specific audiences to be targeted on a geographical basis. The many and varied periodicals, most of which deal with specialised interests, mean that people can be reached by their occupations, hobbies or other interests.

By identifying the right publications for employer or client material, public relations can be a cost-effective service. Not pestering journalists who are not interested, not filling up their in-trays with unwanted material, and instead providing specifically targeted and relevant material will improve not only the relationship with the practitioner but also their success rate. It is not simply a case of using the printed word for messages to specialist audiences. Newspapers survive as a significant medium in the age of broadcasting because of the inelasticity of air time. Even a 30-minute broadcast news bulletin will carry fewer items than a tabloid daily paper. A 30-minute news bulletin, such as ITN's *News at Ten* has an average of just 11 stories each evening, while a quality broadsheet newspaper, such as the *Daily Telegraph*, will have as many on just two pages. Each item broadcast will merit a few sentences, rather than the more extensive coverage afforded by the printed media.

Few countries have such a diverse printed media as the UK. Those countries which have a limited national press and place greater emphasis on regional press include the US, Germany and Spain. The wide range of specialised publications produced in the UK includes many with a truly international readership, reflecting both widespread use of English and the role of the language as the international language in some industries, such as aviation. This can provide an advantage if a client or employer has a product which needs to be marketed internationally.

The main areas of the press are now reviewed.

General press

The term 'general press' covers any newspaper which is not aimed at a specialised audience. They define their audience primarily by their circulation area, which can be wide in the case of the London-based daily and Sunday newspapers. There is also a more subtle breakdown of the audience by class, intellect, political persuasion and, to a lesser extent, degree of affluence.

It is also possible to attribute general press characteristics to some periodicals, such as *Living*, and even those magazines which are aimed mainly at women. This is because their readership covers a wide variety of occupations and interests and is reflected in a varied content from which the main omission is the absence of news and news-related features. Some include features on personal finance, motoring and travel, as well as those on fashion, health, beauty and home interests which have been their traditional mainstay.

Newspapers do not ignore specialised interests completely. Most have columns given over to motoring, gardening, travel, finance and books, for example. Nevertheless, they do so only to the extent that the general reader with a passing interest in such matters is concerned. The motoring enthusiast will find the general press coverage provides earlier news about developments. A banker will note the news coverage of the general press, but augment it with publications more attuned to his or her specific interests. The *Financial Times* is a hybrid, providing quality financial and business coverage, but also covering other items which one would find in general newspapers, such as political news, motoring and personal finance columns aimed at readers as consumers rather than providers.

For material to be accepted by the newspapers, the editorial team has to be convinced that it will be of interest to a significant proportion of their readers.

National and regional press

There is a tendency to consider the 'national' press in the UK as being the London-based morning and Sunday newspapers. This overlooks the Edinburgh, Glasgow and Cardiff-based morning and Sunday newspapers which regard themselves as the 'national' press for Scotland and Wales. In Scotland the indigenous newspapers include both the *Scottish Daily Express* and the *Scottish Daily Mail*. By contrast, the Belfast newspapers are regarded as regional, because Northern Ireland is a province.

Regional press consists of the morning and the few Sunday newspapers published outside London, Edinburgh, Glasgow and Cardiff; in Scotland it includes the Aberdeen and Dundee morning newspapers. Most regional papers carry international and national news as well as regional and local news, but whenever possible news and features attempt to look at national issues in terms of their impact on the region and, of course, their readers.

Regional morning newspapers usually have an evening newspaper as a stablemate, but there are many cities which have evening newspapers without a morning counterpart. Towns and cities without a morning newspaper but which do have an evening newspaper include Manchester (since *The Guardian* departed that city for London many years ago), Swansea, Bath, Peterborough and York. Although most evening newspapers carry international and national news, their focus is more localised than that of the morning newspapers.

The London newspapers have strong editorial teams which will include specialist writers as well as general reporters, and also have their own overseas correspondents in the most important overseas cities. Augmenting the work of their own journalists will be material from the large press agencies.

Regional newspapers with small circulations and limited budgets often will give a single journalist several 'specialisations', although wiser editors endeavour to ensure that these are mutually compatible, such as combining transport and defence, for example, or business and economics, or education and local government. Few have any overseas correspondents, and for this reason such newspapers make much greater use of press agency material. The proprietors of chains of regional newspapers, such as Thomson Regional Newspapers, often provide some material centrally, usually including financial news. Some specialised freelance journalists provide material for several newspapers on a syndicated basis.

The revenue of these newspapers is a combination of advertising and the cover price. Advertising revenue is important to all of them, but especially for the heavier or 'quality' newspapers, where it usually accounts for 75 per cent of revenue when set against their normal cover price.

Local newspapers

Most local newspapers are published weekly, although a few appear twice weekly and there are some fortnightly publications. To ensure the economies of scale while maintaining the local links which their readers demand, many local newspapers are published 'in series', so that one newspaper will appear in each of the towns and villages it serves with a distinctive local name, and much of the editorial will be changed to reflect this.

Local newspapers can be divided into the traditional 'paid-for' publications and the more recent 'freesheets', supported entirely by advertising. These are augmented in some areas by community newspapers, sometimes run by volunteers, but sometimes inspired by the local authority. The freesheets will often have much less editorial material than the paid-for newspapers; compared to the 45–55 per cent editorial material of a typical paid-for newspaper, a freesheet may have just 10 per cent editorial, or less.

Local newspapers have very small editorial teams, and even on a paid-for newspaper a staff of six or less is not uncommon. Staffing levels on the freesheets are lower still. While some of the journalists may be able to develop a specialisation, the usual practice is for them to tackle any story which demands attention. In a typical example, one of the larger and better-staffed local newspapers, a reporter who wanted to develop as a sports reporter was encouraged to do so, but also had to cover a particular district within the paper's circulation area.

Local newspapers place a great reliance on a network of unpaid contributors, who provide news of local events and organisations, and sometimes will even write about a pet interest, such as nature notes or country walks.

Most journalists feel that the great national daily newspapers are the most important. In one sense this is true. A report or an interview in the *Wall Street Journal* may be mentioned in a newspaper or in a broadcast news or current affairs programme. Abroad, overseas broadcasters might refer to the London *Times* or the London *Financial Times*. They would not refer to the

Hobbiton Weekly Advertiser. On the other hand, many members of the public pay more attention to their local newspapers than to national newspapers and, of course, the local newspaper will often remain in the home all week, until it is replaced by the following week's issue.

Press agencies

The Press Association (PA) and Reuters are the major press agencies based in the UK. The PA was founded to provide a service to Britain's newspapers, and was at one time owned by many of them. Traditionally, PA has been more concerned with UK news and Reuters with international news.

There are two other types of press agency which it is important to be aware of. The first of these is the locally based press or news agency, which provides cover in an area for any newspaper without a presence there. Even the big national newspapers no longer have reporters in every major city, and rely on the local news agencies to fill the gap. National newspapers are not, however, the sole clients of the local agency. Sometimes locally based regional newspapers take their material. At other times, they will be working for regional newspapers in another part of the country. For example, if a Scottish family were involved in an accident while on holiday in the West Country, a local news agency would provide a report and photographs for the newspapers in Scotland.

Locally based news agencies have journalists and press photographers, with the latter often being available for commissions by organisations or PR consultancies. When a photographer who understands the press and the needs of picture editors is required, such agencies are often a good place to look.

The other kind of news agency is the overseas agency with a presence in the UK. If a British story is of interest in the US, for example, agencies such as UPI or, in the case of a financial story, AP-Dow Jones, will make sure that the relevant American newspapers receive it.

Agencies are interested in news from companies. Local news agencies will be interested in local organisations, while overseas agencies will be interested if the company has business interests in their home country, or has taken a decision which will affect their home country. The larger British agencies are another means of disseminating a message.

All of these agencies work for the newspapers which employ them, not for companies. The exceptions are the news release distribution companies such as Two Ten Communications, which can be used to distribute press releases to the daily and Sunday newspapers. Not every newspaper accepts Two Ten's wire service, and even those that do realise that it is subscriber-driven. Nevertheless, it is a useful support system, especially if a story is being released as quickly as possible.

Consumer periodicals

As mentioned, most women's interest magazines, and even others such as the county magazines found in the more affluent rural and suburban areas, can be regarded as part of the general press. Most of these publications are paid-for, although there are a few which are supported entirely by advertising and are delivered free to the residents of affluent suburbs.

True editorial coverage of new products is difficult to achieve in such publications. Providing facilities for a travel writer could result in coverage for a destination or a cruise line, for example. Many of these publications, and especially those handling women's interests, have their editorial content planned far in advance, with deadlines for the Christmas issues often as early as August.

The main obstacle for editorial coverage is that many of these publications either favour advertorial, or use some other form of linkage which means that the advertiser benefits most. Some publications sold in supermarkets have editions for different chains, so that the editorial strongly favours the products sold in the particular supermarket chain.

Specialised periodicals

Specialised publications or periodicals cover a wide variety of activities. They include trade and professional publications and publications concerned with hobbies and interests. Sometimes such publications straddle these different markets, as happens with *Modern Railways* which is read by enthusiasts and by those working in the industry. There are also many academic publications.

The format of such publications can vary from newspaper format through to glossy magazine. The frequency of publication can also vary, from daily in the case of the newspaper *Lloyds List*, through weekly, as with *The Grocer* and *Flight International*, to monthly or quarterly.

Content ranges from weekly publications carrying in-depth specialist content to monthly publications, which sometimes carry news, and sometimes not. The news is often of a specialised nature, such as the number of recent deliveries of railway rolling stock, or the departure of a key figure in an industry.

Most of the directories of the media, such as *PR Planner*, code publications so that news, details of new products, book reviews, appointments, photographs and so on can be targeted. As a rule, any publication which appears less frequently than monthly is unlikely to be interested in news material, and this applies especially to academic publications.

Periodicals can be sold over the counter, paid for by subscription only, be given as one of the benefits of belonging to a club or professional institute, or provided free, with their costs met by their advertising revenue. The variations can encompass more than one of these.

Most have small editorial teams, and augment these efforts by freelance contributions solicited from prominent people within the activity being covered. The best, such as *Flight International* and *The Grocer*, have high editorial standards, and in the case of the former, there is a network of overseas correspondents.

Academic publications will often have a part-time editor, who might be supported by a team of assessors, and the content will often consist of papers contributed by leading academics or researchers. These contributions are seldom paid-for. Some smaller periodicals are basically one-man bands, and some will be swayed by the opinions of their advertisers. Some will refuse material from companies which do not advertise with them, and this is true of some regional business magazines. It is not uncommon for local chamber of commerce publications to carry news only about their member companies.

Some go as far as the magazine *Process Products*, which offers editorial space to anyone willing to pay for it, telling the potential purchaser of this service that the 'editor's right to discard or cut your copy is gone forever'. The problem is that this is a small and specialised market, and so a practice which is likely to result in dull or flabby editorial goes unchallenged by a competitor.

Far more exacting standards are expected in magazines which cover sectors in which there is intense interest, such as aviation. In specialised fields, the number of enthusiasts might have much to do in raising editorial standards and ensuring editorial competitiveness.

9

Why: press relations – a means to an end

There is the story about a British admiral who, in the early years of the present century walked into a gunnery class. Turning to a nervous young midshipman he asked him what was the purpose of gunnery. 'To fire the gun, sir!' was the reply. The admiral's face purpled, and no doubt the midshipman's paled, and he bellowed: 'Boy, the purpose of gunnery is to hit the target!'

Similarly the purpose of press relations is not to issue press releases or handle enquiries from journalists, or even to generate a massive pile of press cuttings. The true purpose of press relations is to enhance the reputation of an organisation and its products, and to influence and inform the target audiences.

Generally, businesses use public relations for a number of specific reasons, and usually in this order of importance:

- improving company or brand image
- higher (and better) media profile
- changing the attitudes of target audiences (such as customers)
- improving relationships with the community

- increasing their market share
- influencing government policy at local, national or international level
- improving communications with investors and their advisers
- improving industrial relations.

While media relations seems to come second, in reality all of these objectives can be assisted to some extent by more favourable media coverage. Good editorial comment on a company's financial performance will do more for the confidence of private investors and institutional fund managers than a glossy annual report will ever do. After all, for many investors the annual report is the corporate equivalent of a car brochure, and prospective buyers will be interested to know how a motoring correspondent found a particular car.

Even though employee communications programmes are essential, good media coverage will also help to influence employee attitudes. Often many employees will learn most about developments from the newspapers. While employee communications are trusted in good companies, employees still place great store by the judgements of journalists.

Of course, many in business, and in other activities as well, like the idea of press relations for the 'free' publicity it provides. However, good media coverage is not free. This is not because of the growth of advertorial or colour separation charges, but because good-quality PR professionals are seldom cheap. They also need good equipment, and need to spend money on support services.

The quality of press relations is even more important than the quantity. Success may lie sometimes in not having press coverage at all.

In one particular case, a man with a gun entered a public house, threatening customers and staff before he could be cornered by the police and arrested. The press office at the brewery worked hard to persuade the press that there was no need to mention the brewery's name in their reports, and few did. The brewery wished to distance itself from the publicity, and the press generally accepted that the name of the brewery was incidental. Obviously the name of the public house had to be reported.

Matching the media

Truly effective press relations starts with effective targeting. There is no point in sending a technical story to a general newspaper, or a photograph of a victorious works football team to a periodical which only carries product news. A local weekly newspaper might be interested in the latter story, and the periodical might find the former interesting.

The process of matching a client or employer to the media available is relatively simple. There are four questions to answer:

● What is the function of the organisation?
● Which audiences are essential to its success?
● What messages does it wish to convey?
● Which media are available for this?

Function

An organisation's function will affect its media exposure considerably. In companies such as the P&O Group, the press relations demands of its operating divisions vary enormously. The high-profile cruises and passenger ferries require the most support. This reflects the fragmented market, with literally tens of thousands of individual customers booking through thousands of travel agents. The cargo ships and bulk carriers require less, because they have fewer customers, with less than 20 worldwide for the fleet of gas carriers. People moving freight are less concerned about who carries their goods than people are when making their holiday arrangements, when they might have a preference for one cruise ship over another.

A manufacturer of motor components would have a lower profile and fewer customers to influence than the manufacturer of the end product, the motor car itself. There is more general interest in a new model from a motor car manufacturer than from the manufacturer of commercial vehicles.

Audiences

As well as understanding the organisation's activities, it is important to understand the audience. The P&O example mentioned shows that the traveller is as important as the travel agent. In the case of general cargo operations, the freight forwarder or shipping agent is probably more important than the exporter or importer, but in the case of a large bulk carrier, the broker handling the charter arrangements will need consideration.

The manufacturer of components only needs to reach distributors and the general public if these are sold under the firm's own branding. In many cases, their audience is the small number of motor manufacturers, who will supply the components with their own branding through their own distributors. It is the manufacturer who has to convince the general public, fleet managers and distributors of the worth of the new car. Even then, their distributors usually have a more restrictive link with the motor manufacturer than the travel agent would have with a tour operator, ferry company or cruise line. Commercial vehicle manufacturers also have distributors, but in reaching the purchaser, they may have a limited audience or a very fragmented one, depending on the size of vehicle and its degree of specialisation.

Other audiences are important apart from prospective customers and distributors. Organisations need to influence shareholders, local and central government, and the communities in which they are based, as well as prospective employees and even suppliers.

Messages

Because audiences can be diverse, most organisations will have more than one message to convey. Prospective shareholders will want to be assured about viability, employees about security, and customers about the nature and quality of the product. The old salesman's cliché about 'selling the sizzle and not the steak' also has much truth. The sizzle and aroma of cooking has a greater impact than the sight of a piece of raw meat.

In the case of P&O cruises, the message could not be simply 'cruise P&O', still less 'have a cruising holiday'. The message had to convey the benefits of cruising as opposed to other holidays, so the facilities of the ship and the itinerary need emphasis. In contrast, people travelling by ferry are most interested in the route, the schedules and the fares.

Freight forwarders and other agents would be interested in the capacity of a cargo ship, its ability to handle awkward loads, and the schedule.

Travel agents would want the same information as their customers so that they could emphasise the benefits to them. In addition, they would want to know about their own margins, any special incentives, and the availability of the product.

The media

Messages have to be tailored to the wide variety of media available, being clear about the target audience. For example, periodicals which cover the charities field are fine to pass on a worthwhile experience, or air a grievance, but will not help in fund-raising.

If a company is preoccupied with the specialised press this may be effective in communicating to its peers and distributors, but overlooks the need to attract the attention of decision-makers among the end-users. If a priority was to attract prospective purchasers into the dealers, and obtain enquiries to be followed up by the sales team, change of media and a different emphasis in press releases and articles or case histories could achieve this. Some media feature reader-enquiry cards, which means that as well as sending prospective purchasers a brochure and the name of the local dealer, the dealer would also receive the enquiry, and pursue it; this would improve the manufacturer's relationships with its dealers.

The key to effective use of the media is to:

- Use the specialised media for the sector to announce developments and air matters of interest.
- Use academic or technical publications to enhance the reputation of staff and to discover if research is being duplicated elsewhere which could lead to collaboration.
- Use other specialised media to interest distributors, such as travel agents or retailers.
- Use national press to announce major investments, new products if these are of sufficient interest (which in the case of many industrial and consumer products, is very rare), and company results if quoted on the Stock Exchange. Research, campaigns, events and crisis management are other areas to utilise the nationals.
- Regional newspapers will often be interested if they can be given the regional angle.
- Local newspapers will be interested in the activities of companies in their area, not least because it affects the prosperity of the neighbourhood. Companies which regard an industrial dispute as nobody's business but their own risk damaging their image among the local community, including prospective employees and potential customers.

The press will usually be more interested in a major issue affecting an industry or a charity, or the results of research which throw light on public attitudes or behaviour than in the straightforward promotion of a product or a campaign. Such material can do much to develop a high level of respect and co-operation with target journalists.

Pressure on newspaper space is often considerable. Newspapers are not elastic. On a busy news day, a story which might otherwise have received extensive coverage in a prominent position will get less space, and stories which might have received a brief mention might have to be passed over.

Promoting the product

Genuinely new and different products of interest to the general reader will usually receive the coverage they deserve, and many specialised products will receive coverage in specialist periodicals. Nevertheless, not every product is new and exciting. Many are simply another brand's interpretation of an idea.

Existing products which have remained much the same for many years, may also need the use of different techniques to give coverage.

Advertorial

Editorial space linked to advertising is often called advertorial. An advertisement of a certain size will result in an agreed amount of editorial being run. Sometimes the newspaper or magazine editor will provide a journalist to write the editorial, but it is more usual for this to be provided by the PR function or consultancy. This crosses a difficult boundary, and many journalists feel it compromises editorial independence.

An advertorial can be a form of paid-for editorial without an accompanying advertisement being placed. Many shopping or restaurant-guide features amount to this. In a local or regional newspaper, a special feature will cover the shopping opportunities in a particular district. The shops and restaurants mentioned are those who have paid for the privilege.

Many regional business publications also allow themselves to be heavily influenced in their editorial judgements by their advertisers. Many will not publish news or features which do not concern their advertisers. This practice has also crept into some regional and national newspapers which will publish special supplements, heavily supported by advertising. Often, the only time a non-advertiser can expect an editorial mention will be if they are responsible for such a major development in their sector that it is impossible for the person editing the supplement to ignore them completely.

There are other occasions when advertorial can be useful. A

building society, opening a new branch in the suburb of a major city, used advertorial in the two local weekly newspapers. The logic was that the target audience were likely to read these because of their strong circulation in the suburb in question. The advertorial concentrated on the strength of the society and its development, as well as the special features of its products.

Advertorial can help break into the media when genuine editorial interest is low, but professional practitioners will always prefer to win editorial space on the merit of a news story or a background feature, obtaining good coverage after passing objective editorial scrutiny.

Much really depends on the value set by publishers on the quality of their newspapers or periodicals. Appointments columns should be free editorial selected on their news value rather than paid-for advertising. The trend started in Dublin and has spread to the UK, especially Scotland. PR people have generally resisted paying for appointments, which is easy to do since rarely does a new appointment or promotion automatically mean more business enquiries, unlike a new product.

Nevertheless, not all appointments stories are sent to the press by PR departments. The result has been that the appointments columns, especially in Scotland, have ceased to contain stories of the appointment of senior people to Scottish business, and instead have been filled by details of new sales representatives and area managers. No longer do these columns keep the business community abreast of worthwhile changes, but at least anyone interested now knows who to approach for double glazing.

Colour separation charges

Many trade publications will offer to run a colour picture alongside a product story if the costs of separations are paid for by the company. This is a further blurring of the distinction between editorial and advertising which has prompted action by the IPR. At present, colour separations cost between £12 and £40 to produce, but publications have been charging between £40 and £350. The Periodical Publishers' Association guidelines provide that the words 'advertisement', 'advertising' or 'promotion' should identify any paid-for editorial space. When illustrations have been paid for, this should also be made clear.

The problem is that a colour photograph is more likely to catch the eye of the reader. Nevertheless, this is something which should be resisted.

Newspaper and magazine competitions

Another means of breaking into areas closed to straightforward editorial is the reader competition. Competitions are being used increasingly by motor-car manufacturers. Giving away five or six cars over a week in a daily newspaper can result in extensive coverage, often with the competition mentioned on the front page, and with coverage on the editorial pages. This is more likely to be noticed than advertising, especially if the readers have to collect tokens so that they can enter the competition.

Promotional offers

Special promotional offers, exclusively for the readers of a particular newspaper or magazine, have also become increasingly common in recent years. Often these will also require readers to collect tokens over a period, which has the double benefit of encouraging people to take every issue of the publication, and ensuring that the company behind the special offer receives repeated publicity in each issue.

Many of these offers are self-financing. For example, a ferry company offering free or discounted return passages will hope to make a profit on duty free and other sales during the crossing. Restaurants offering two meals for the price of one will do this in the expectation that most customers will also be spending on wine and other drinks. For the same reason, free hotel accommodation is usually subject to the condition that all meals are taken in the hotel restaurant.

P&O found that special reader offers were of significance in promoting cruising to a wider audience. A newspaper readers' cruise, in conjunction with a local travel agent, gave the newspaper and the shipping company value, with editorial coverage of local people on holiday. The offer received extensive coverage for several weeks while bookings were being sought. Readers like to think that they will be going with people from their area or people with similar interests. If members of the editorial team are known to be accompanying the holiday, this is an added attraction, reflecting the often close relationship between many publications and their readership.

Sponsorship

There is a growing use of sponsorship for programmes on independent radio and television. Sponsorship is also becoming more widespread in newspapers and magazines, the difference being that none of the controls exercised over radio and television sponsorship is present in the printed media. Sponsors of broadcast programmes cannot influence the producers' judgement or interfere in editorial decisions, and should not feature in the broadcast. This allows credit-card companies and football-pools promoters to sponsor travel programmes, but the former would not be allowed to sponsor a personal-finance programme (still less one on consumer debt), and the latter would not be able to sponsor a programme on football.

Special editions of some consumer magazines prepared especially for individual supermarket chains are also a form of sponsorship.

Banks sponsor business supplements in regional newspapers, as well as special supplements for certain audiences, such as students. In both cases there is a direct commercial connection.

The practice can influence editorial and even when it does not, many readers have their perception of the editorial influenced, believing that it is less impartial than it should be.

Public relations versus paid-for editorial

Editorial integrity has become a major issue not only for the media, but for PR practitioners. Editorial coverage is important because people seldom buy publications for the advertising, and the perceived impartiality of the journalists plays an important role in influencing the readers. Paying for coverage may be worthwhile in some cases, if it links to marketing considerations.

During the late 1970s, Cunard threatened to stop advertising cruises in *The Times* and *The Sunday Times* unless its editorial coverage was improved. *The Times* carried the story on the front page as a defiant declaration of editorial independence and integrity. Some at P&O had been hinting at a similar strategy before this. Managements, or clients, are always more aware of a competitor's press coverage than of their own! The more coverage people receive, the more they expect, even during quieter periods when their organisation has little worth saying, and even less worth printing.

10

News, features and more

People buy newspapers primarily for their news content. Nevertheless, over the years, newspapers have come to include a selection of articles, more usually referred to as features material, while some periodicals have little or no news content.

Employers and clients will appreciate news coverage presenting them in a good light. Yet successful organisations do not simply make the news, even if it is in a limited way within a specialised field or a confined geographical area. Really successful organisations also feature in articles, whether it be interviews with important members of the management team, a review or critique of a product, which includes much travel writing with the destination as the product, or in a feature on a development within their sector.

Photographs have their part to play. Pictures draw the eye to part of the page as well as simply illustrating a point. Colour provides additional appeal and extra depth. Imagine having to use words alone to describe a new car in such a way that the interested reader would be able to identify it in the street. Photographs of happy, smiling consumers cannot illustrate a mortgage or a life-assurance policy. Nevertheless, even financial institutions make considerable use of photography, using up-to-date photographs of their senior people, of typical branches and historical material. The latter can help to portray the organisation in a certain way showing both a concern for the past as well as the stability and longevity so important in this sphere.

News

Clients or employers often underrate or exaggerate the news value of a development, as they cannot regard it objectively. Modesty can cause people to underestimate the news value of a speech or a paper they are presenting. Objectivity is the most important discipline in assessing news value; superlatives such as 'biggest', 'smallest', 'best', 'first' or 'longest' should be avoided, as should stating a company's product is better than that of a named competitor. Genuine firsts or bests are rare. Even in technical publications, the journalists are rarely in a position to be so sure about such claims themselves, and so, for their own professional credibility, they delete them.

Some journalists will make comparisons of products and recommend the product which they perceive as being best value, especially on the consumer pages of the general press, including the personal-finance columns, while the Consumers' Association magazine *Which?* employs teams of testers and researchers. Most publications do not have this type of support.

News implies that something is new, and different. The reason why newspapers are more likely to write about railway delays or road accidents is because on-time arrivals and safe travel are the expected norm. During the early 1970s, when industrial disputes were rife in Britain's ports and hardly a day passed without one or more disputes, the shipping and insurance daily newspaper, *Lloyds List*, once ran a small news item to the effect that there had been no industrial disputes in the Port of Liverpool the previous day! Good news for once, but damaging to the reputation of the port.

News can be:

- a new product
- an important new contract

- a senior appointment
- improved results
- major investments
- a major campaign or project
- research findings
- an acquisition or a merger
- a major staff success, perhaps fund-raising for a charity.

Not all of these will have equal weight. Whether or not the general press will be interested will depend on the importance of a new product or a new contract. Money speaks volumes to journalists, because this is an objective measure of the importance of a new contract or a major investment by your employer or client. Newspapers which are regional or local will find news arising in their circulation area to be more relevant.

The appeal to the reader is what matters. A new office desk will be of interest only to specialised periodicals unless, of course, it has some feature which makes it dramatically different from anything which has gone before. A new car from a major manufacturer might have some general news interest, but unless it is extra-special in some way, any significant coverage will have to await its turn in the regular motoring columns. The specialised motoring press would be likely to cover this.

Timing news

Newspapers have a standard format for each issue. On a quiet news day, a story might be used which on another day would not stand a chance. To some extent, this is a matter of luck, but avoid days when a competitor might be making an announcement or when there is some major event, such as the State Opening of Parliament.

Releasing news during periods when the press could be short of stories, such as the period between Christmas and the New Year, may also be fruitful, but it can also mean that people are not bothering too much with the newspapers either. Timing stories so that they can break over the weekend, ready for

Monday morning's newspapers can be successful, especially for stories concerning the work of charities and for others which may involve the journalists in some additional investigation and reporting of their own, but it will depend for its success on there being a good weekend duty press officer.

Features

Features can support news coverage, providing background on developments, or be part of a regular series, such as motoring, gardening or travel. Features coverage can be a vehicle for advertising.

There are also opportunities for 'think pieces', with prominent people or experts in a particular field writing articles on matters about which they have an authoritative view. In the general press, such pieces are concerned with economics or health matters, and occasionally politics, but in the specialised periodicals, editors may invite contributions from those running businesses which are prominent in their field. The public relations practitioner can ghost such pieces for a client or employer.

Interviews with prominent people often provide good features material (see Chapter 12). Specialised periodicals are often happy to carry features dealing with the progress of a new project or innovation. This can be an invaluable means of keeping a new business development in the press, long after the initial news value has died down.

Features do more than expand the news coverage: they also prolong press interest. It is difficult to maintain the news value of an existing product or service. Production milestones, the millionth passenger to use a service, or major new contracts can maintain interest; but such stories have their limitations.

However, coverage in any regular review or survey is vital. For a company in the holiday business, journalists writing for the travel columns, and those broadcasting on holidays as well, must be aware of the company's products and its latest prices, and also have the opportunity of sampling these. The same goes for companies in other fields, with motor manufacturers getting their share of new car road tests in the motoring columns.

To stimulate coverage in regional and local newspapers, freelance writers with syndicated columns could be invited to test the product. Alternatively, local dealers or distributors could make their test cars available to the motoring writer on the regional or local newspaper.

Some regional and local newspapers also appreciate PR-generated features material, without necessarily expecting it to be accompanied by advertising, on condition that it is not perceived as being a selling piece. Such material can be used to stimulate awareness of the local presence and enhance the image of the local manager as an expert in the field. Unless the features article is about a specific experience discovered by the organisation, newspapers may object to references to the company or to its own products in the article. The whole ethos of such articles is that of providing impartial expert advice, and the credit to the organisation comes from being associated with the writer in the byline.

Photographs

Good photography means photographs which are usable by the press, and which reflect to the advantage of a client or employer.

Marketing-led photography of brochures and advertising usually centres on a product, while newspapers generally prefer action shots. Instead of sterile product shots it will pay dividends to invest in a photographic session with models using the product.

Avoid stereotypes, however. Models do not have to be any particular colour or sex, secretaries do not have to be women, and housework is no longer a female preserve. Members of staff may be used.

Photographs can be tailored to a wider audience by dressing models in white coats for laboratory workers, doctors or veterinary surgeons, brown or blue coats for a warehouse or industrial application, and in suits for a variety of applications. Newspapers hate the sort of school-photograph line up. People should be in workaday situations which say something about the organisation's activities. This also works with photographs of individuals, such as putting an airline boss into the captain's seat on an aircraft, or having a shipping company chairman on the bridge of a ship.

Checked suits and ties with an intricate pattern may cause problems with colour reproduction. An unusual angle may provide an interesting photograph, such as a heavy load suspended in mid-air.

A good photographer will be able to offer a great deal of invaluable advice on interpreting client needs in a way which is appreciated by newspaper picture editors. Such people also understand the importance of keeping to tight deadlines and are equipped to meet these.

Photographers differ widely, for they specialise. Those whose prime activity consists of wedding photography may not be equipped to provide imaginative architectural shots.

Good photography is not necessarily the most expensive. Several directories list photographers and give details of their specialisations. If photography is needed in a town many miles from headquarters, avoid paying travelling expenses and subsistence: local news and pictures agencies are often available for PR commissions.

Media requirements govern whether colour transparencies or negatives, or black-and-white negatives and prints are needed.

Newspaper photographers work quickly and often without supervision. They are accustomed to catching the moment as the VIP steps off the train. Other types of PR photography are more difficult to arrange. Photographs of a new product, the interior of new premises or a group shot of the board will often require time to be spent on lighting, so that not only does everything look good, but disconcerting areas of shadow or reflections are avoided.

A photographic checklist

There are a few details to bear in mind when commissioning photographs, sending them to the press and maintaining a collection. These include:

- Always caption photographs on the back.
- Keep a record of the photographer with the reference number so re-ordering is simple.
- Obtain special storage files for colour transparencies.
- If black-and-white photographs are needed as well as colour, use black-and-white negative film in addition to colour negatives or transparencies. Many newspapers will accept colour prints but a colour transparency gives better reproduction. Colour printed in black and white is much better today than used to be the case, but a black-and-white print will still be crisper and offer better contrast.
- For portrait photographs, black-and-white or colour prints as small as 5 × 4 inches will suffice, but otherwise have a minimum size of 8 × 6 inches or, even better, 10 × 8 inches.
- While the quality of 35mm transparencies is much improved today, it is still worth considering a larger format if a substantial enlargement is contemplated.
- Always have cardboard-backed envelopes in stock to avoid photographs and transparencies being bent in the post.

Photographers hold the copyright in their work, and it is important to be clear about the cost of subsequent reprints. Some public relations people endeavour to buy the copyright outright when commissioning the photographer, or after they have seen either proof prints or a contact print and can decide which shots they wish to use. If a set of photographs plus a few spares for record purposes for a press release is required, paying the cost of the session and the prints will be less expensive. If varied and extensive use of material is necessary, then it may be worthwhile to buy the copyright.

11

How: writing for the press

Many PR people spend most of their time writing material which is intended for the press, either drafting press releases, writing features material or accurate and interesting photograph captions.

Collaboration may be required to clear some kinds of information before it is sent out. Press releases on new products will be the preserve of the marketing director, although this responsibility might be delegated to a manager in the appropriate department. Releases on a company's annual results will have to be cleared with the chairman, chief executive and finance director.

An agreed decision-making procedure is needed which can authorise press releases quickly, involving as few people as possible.

Press releases

Only one press release in ten is published by any newspaper, and the proportion which are accepted by a broad spectrum of the press is lower still.

There are three reasons for this high failure rate:

- A release may not contain news, or if it does, it is so insignificant or so specialised that no one is interested except the issuer.
- Many releases are badly written, include too much technical material and jargon, and hide the real story deep in the body of the release. This is the most common reason for a release failure.
- Many releases are not targeted accurately and are sent with a scatter-gun approach to all contacts on the media list.

Successful press releases follow certain rules:

- A single A4 page is the ideal length.
- Unnecessary and pointless phrases such as 'announces' or 'is pleased to announce' should be avoided.
- Two inches should be left at the top for the newspaper sub-editor to write instructions to the printer and to add a headline. There should be a one-and-a-half inch left-hand margin for the editor's amendments and text should be double-spaced.
- Always date the release at the top, so that the news editor can see that the story is current.
- A short, eye-catching headline is needed to attract the attention of a busy news editor.
- The main facts must be included in a short first paragraph. A busy sub-editor will cut from the bottom. The ideal release should still be able to work if only the first paragraph is printed.
- Quotes should be included, attributed to a named senior individual for impact; if the target press are local, the branch manager will be more appropriate.
- Each paragraph should be no more than three sentences, with just one or two for the first paragraph.
- Too much detail detracts from impact, but significant points must be included: accuracy is paramount.
- Good journalistic style is better than legal niceties.
- Jargon should be avoided whenever possible, especially when writing for the general press.

- Superlatives should not be included, such as 'best', 'first' or 'excellent'.
- A brief concluding statement about the organisation's activities should be included if it is not well known.
- The release should finish with 'ENDS' to avoid confusion.
- A contact name and both daytime and out-of-hours telephone numbers should be included at the foot of the release.
- Several versions of the same release may be provided for different audiences and the publications which reach them. Technical publications might appreciate a longer version of the release, perhaps with a data or specification sheet.
- If a good photograph adds to the story, make sure one is provided, suitably captioned, for those publications which use photographs.
- If a brochure or price list might also help, include these items.
- A sample of the product would be useful if it is a practical proposition to offer this. This works well for foodstuffs, and is essential for such items as books, video material and recorded music.
- When a journalist is likely to need time to research and write an important story, allow extra time for this, using an embargo to reduce the chance of the story breaking too early. Head the press release:

   'EMBARGO: Not for publication or broadcast before XX.XX hours, XXday, XXdate'.

- Embargoes may need to be flexible. A Sunday-morning story can be allowed in a Saturday-evening newspaper, especially if the story is national and the evening paper is in a town where the company has head offices or a major factory.

An example of the way in which different versions of a press release can work arose when a Scottish firm of investment managers was raising funds for an Oxford college. The story was a UK national story to attract the main body of investors, an Oxford story because of the target, and a Scottish success story because of the company's location. Usually such variations can be handled easily simply by changing the introductory paragraph, but quotes may also need amendment or be attributed to a different individual.

Attention to such small details will take a little extra time, but will improve the effectiveness of each press release.

Distribution

Mailing lists must be kept up to date. Organisations may need several. A bank will need one list for journalists dealing with personal finance, another for those interested in finance for businesses, a third for economics correspondents, and a fourth for its own financial results. Further lists will be needed if it localises press releases to boost the profile of its branches. Other sectors will want to have lists for newspapers read by their customers, for magazines read by their distributors, and so on.

The importance of up-to-date mailing lists cannot be over-emphasised. As part of an in-house training session at the Royal Bank of Scotland, the Chief Press Officer asked the business editor of *The Scotsman* for the discarded envelopes from one morning's mail. A large black plastic bin liner was emptied on to the table, covering it with opened envelopes. On inspection most of these were not for the current editorial team on the newspaper; many were not even for their immediate predecessors, and a few were for people who had left five or more years earlier, or even for people who had died.

If organisations persist with one mailing list every journalist gets everything. Often they will not be interested, and, if too few releases are relevant, they will become accustomed to tossing anything from that company or agency into the waste-paper basket.

Features

Most features will be written by journalists working either as freelances or as staff members of a particular publication. They will sometimes ask for help when researching a feature, and on occasion they might ask for an interview with someone within the organisation. Such meetings will be covered in Chapter 12.

General rules for the successful handling of enquiries are set out below:

- Information requested must be provided as quickly as possible, and within the deadline set by the journalist.
- Interviews must be arranged speedily.
- Sufficient time must be allowed for the interview. If a journalist wants 20 minutes, it could take twice as long. A good interview will often stimulate discussion on other areas, and perhaps more than one article will result. Sometimes a journalist will need help with background and jargon will need to be interpreted.
- If it is impossible to help within the time set, this should be admitted at once, so that the journalist can go elsewhere and goodwill is maintained.
- If all goes well, the journalist should have everything needed for the article. This may include facts or figures, photographs, back copies of annual reports, and should be provided by the public relations practitioner.
- An offer to check facts and to be available to answer queries should be made. Keep any comments to facts alone, ignoring the style.
- Asking to see the article before it goes to press often causes offence.

PR features

It is possible to interest journalists in writing an article about an organisation or its work, or an interview with a significant member of the team, but there are many occasions when public relations practitioners are expected to prepare features material. The piece might have a byline, or be unsigned, which happens in many trade publication features. Often, it will be ghost-written on behalf of someone else. The person for whom material is ghosted does not have to be senior, since it could be a feature offered to local newspapers and carrying the name of the company's local branch manager.

The best types of features are those which follow the same rules as the material provided by the publication's own editorial team. The type of material might include:

- reviews of company products or innovations for regular features on the market in trade publications
- authoritative pieces on developments in the industry or sector ghosted for directors or senior managers
- advice pieces, which might have the byline of a senior member of the management for general use, but which can be offered to local newspapers as localised pieces carrying the name of the local branch manager
- review or overview pieces, signed by the company's economist, and offered to the general and specialised press as an alternative to their own specialists.

The general rules are:

- Always have a start, a middle and an end.
- Always write to the length specified by the editor.
- Most readers will decide whether to continue or move on to another item very quickly, so the first paragraph or two will mark the feature as a success or a failure.
- Unless asked specifically to do so, as in a trade-publication review of products in a certain field, or in advertorial, avoid emphasising the company's own products.
- Be objective when writing about industry developments.
- Always have the material typed in double spacing with a wide left-hand margin.
- Provide portrait photographs of the author or product photographs, as appropriate.
- Identify the author's job title.
- Always make sure that the official author is happy with the article: give the author the opportunity to make changes.

When writing advertorial, it should follow the same editorial style as the publication. Do not overbrand. The idea is to produce something which a journalist who is favourable to the product might write and it should appeal to the readers of the publication.

12

How: talking to the press

Contact with journalists is an everyday activity in public relations. Most talking is done over the telephone, but there will be times when this is face to face. Public relations practitioners may also sit in on interviews between your clients or employers and journalists.

The ideal relationship between journalists and public relations practitioners is one based on trust. Efficiency and sensitivity are essential.

The interests of the journalists and the organisation are not necessarily the same. The journalists want facts, information for news items and for feature articles and to have their story accepted by their editor. The organisation wants to be viewed in a good light. Often organisations make the mistake of believing that they can talk to the press only when it suits them, and not at other times. Even if the outcome is likely to be bad news, a willingness to explain will help matters.

Journalists are cynical about those prominent people who are happy to court the press on good days, and will ignore it on days when the going gets difficult. Journalists also resent being telephoned to discover whether or not they have received a particular press release.

Jargon

Much of the jargon of journalism has passed into the language. Some of the more common terms are explained below:

- **Quote**. This is what the journalist wants, the opportunity to quote someone, providing their article with additional authority and authenticity. Ideally, they like to attribute the quote to a named individual such as a director or specialist in a particular field, but a spokesperson is second best, and will sometimes be accepted.

- **On the record**. Speaking to a journalist, remarks are automatically 'on the record', unless prefixed by a qualifying remark.

- **Off the record**. This means that whatever is about to be said should not be quoted, and is for the background information of the journalist. It is important that the intention to go off the record is made clear before making the remarks, and that the journalist agrees to the condition. Remarks cannot be stated as off the record after they have been made, and too much off the record can make an interview useless.

- **Non-attributable**. There are times when someone might be happy to see something reported, but less happy to have their name attributed to the remarks in print. A quote may be attributed to 'industry sources' or 'a senior official'. It may be useful when commenting on a situation affecting an industry sector as a whole, especially if competitors are reluctant to speak. Remarks must be prefixed with this condition, and the journalist must agree, before anyone goes ahead.

- **No comment**. There are still people who believe that this is the right way to address any press enquiry. In practice, it leaves the journalists and their readers to draw their own (usually unfavourable) conclusions. Sometimes comment cannot be made because a matter is *sub judice*, but this must be explained. Customer confidentiality is another example when comment is difficult (see below).

- **Embargo**. See Chapter 11, p. 86.

- **Deadline**. The time at which the story must be ready. When a journalist telephones with a question it is important to find out their deadline. Even if information is not available, a phone call should be made before the deadline expires to explain this. There is no need to be too precise in the explanation: saying that an organisation cannot comment on rumours on the stock markets because the finance director has gone to Bolivia, and no one knows when he or she is coming back, might provide a front-page story, and an end to the press officer's career.

- **Scoop**. A genuine scoop, usually billed as an 'exclusive' is rare these days. Giving one journalist a scoop might be worthwhile on occasion, but it carries with it the danger of offending rival newspapers.

Customer confidentiality is always a difficult matter. One bank press officer sometimes had this problem when journalists telephoned him to discuss a complaint to their newspaper by a customer of the bank. His technique was to explain about customer confidentiality and its importance. He would then offer to discuss the matter fully, and even show the journalist the files, providing that the customer in question provided written permission for the bank to do so. Needless to say, they never did, and the journalist would always drop the story. This technique only works if a complaint to the press is ill-founded. Well-justified complaints were referred to higher management by the press office so that they could be resolved.

Companies negotiating major contracts are often reluctant to say anything worthwhile in advance of the announcement of an agreement. When this is happening, it is advisable for the press office to devise a holding statement with those conducting the negotiations, so that something worthwhile can be given in response to press enquiries.

Meeting the press

Good long-term relationships with journalists are invaluable. Journalists differ, and the public relations practitioner must assess those who are to be trusted, and those who are more reckless. For instance non-attributable and off-the-record quotes should not be offered on first acquaintance.

To lunch or not to lunch?

It has become more difficult to get journalists to attend a lunch simply for the sake of getting to know the press officer, since the pressures on them have grown. Rarely is it worthwhile offering lunch to a general reporter, unless it coincides with an interview with a client or an employer.

The specialised correspondents of the general press and members of the editorial team on specialised periodicals of interest to a client's or employer's activities are a different matter. There are mutual advantages in such meetings as they can tell the press officer their views of the organisation and where they would like to see some improvements. It gives the organisation an insight into outside perceptions and a guide to how to improve press relations in the short term.

It is sometimes possible to arrange lunches where several journalists can meet senior members of the management team. It must be made clear to those being invited that it is nothing more than a 'get to know you' lunch, and that there will be other journalists there. Some will be happy with this, and indeed meeting their peers might be regarded as part of the attraction. Others will express a preference to be lunched on their own, so that they do not have to share any story which arises with their competitors.

Sometimes, managements attempt to 'theme' lunches. This is a good idea if this involves inviting only economics correspondents or the London editors of regional newspapers. It can be a bad idea if it means that the management wishes to talk about a specific subject. Journalists are likely to have their own individual agenda. If the subject is interesting enough to be themed, it does not need to be because the press will be sufficiently interested anyway.

Press interviews

In arranging interviews, it is important to discover the subjects which the journalist wishes to discuss, and also how much time they will need. Such interviews usually run over the allotted time, especially if they go well. Also, events may affect the subjects covered. If a chief executive has agreed to meet a journalist to discuss the company's plans to develop cross-Channel-ferry services and there is a major accident (even to a ship belonging to a competitor) on the previous day, safety instantly comes to the top of the agenda. If there is a major crisis, routine interviews have to be cancelled while the chief executive combats the crisis and fronts a major press conference.

It is important that all press interviews for management and for directors of any organisation have a press officer present. The more senior the individual being interviewed, the more senior the public relations person should be: if it is necessary to intervene, this requires fine judgement and confidence.

The interview can act as a briefing for the public relations function, which is both brought up to date on developments and on the organisation's policies, and how far it is prepared to commit itself publicly, on or off the record. This makes it easier for the public relations function to comment instantly when the question arises again.

Senior people may not know what is going on at the sharp end and the public relations person might have this information to hand, or can undertake to provide this and any other information which the journalist requires.

If there is disagreement over what was and was not said, the public relations practitioner can remind people what was said when they dispute what appears in print. Usually, such disputes are not worth bothering over.

It should be found out in advance not only the reason for the interview, but whether or not the journalist is familiar with the organisation. It can be useful building in time for a preliminary conversation and having background material ready so that the journalist can be brought up to date on developments.

Press conferences and receptions

Press conferences are ideal for events or announcements of major importance. They are not for trivial matters, and once anyone has acquired the reputation of calling a press conference without real justification for it, they will find that attendance dwindles. These events are not for the vanity of directors or senior management, they are for the press.

Press conferences have the advantage of enabling journalists to question senior management or directors on major announcements or developments, and to ensure that everyone has the same consistent replies. Consistency of message is less likely when journalists are spoken to individually. Timing is another important aspect of press conferences, because they all hear the story at the same time. If 20 journalists were to telephone individually, those at the back of the queue would be short of time to research and write their copy.

Conferences are useful for announcing the results of a large publicly quoted company, or for a major investment or other initiative. They can pull together the organisation's reaction to a crisis or major accident. A rehearsal within 24 hours before the conference, with the public relations team adopting the role of journalists and challenging statements by those who will be fronting the press conference is a good idea. In the case of a crisis press conference those facing the press must know the current situation.

In the case of a conference for the annual results of a company, investment analysts should be invited before the press so that financial journalists can quote their reactions.

Press receptions can be a useful way of meeting journalists

informally, especially if any development does not justify a fully-blown press conference. The launch of a new programme of holidays can be an opportunity for travel writers and the travel trade press to be invited to a press reception: it might not justify a press conference.

The main points in organising a press conference or reception are detailed below:

1. Only select and invite those likely to be interested.
2. Let those being invited know the purpose of the event. If many refuse, the event is not worthwhile.
3. Except in a crisis, those invited should be telephoned 24 hours before the event to remind them.
4. All guests should be signed in to provide a record of those attending.
5. Hosts should be kept to the minimum. Anyone who has worked as a journalist will have tales of events where the hosts outnumbered the journalists.
6. Hosts must be briefed on who is attending, and on any likely issues or interests.
7. For press conferences, speakers should rehearse the day before.
8. Only have hosts with a strong sense of discretion.
9. A programme, stating starting and finishing time, is useful. Lunchtime events should end by 2.30pm, so that busy journalists can get away.
10. Journalists unable to attend should have material distributed at the function sent to them as a courtesy, and for information.
11. Timing must be convenient for those being invited. Sunday-newspaper journalists do not work on Mondays. Weekly trade and local newspapers usually go to press on Wednesdays, which is a busy day as a result. Morning-newspaper journalists often start work late in the morning. Evening-newspaper journalists often finish work (especially outside London) by 4.00pm.

Clashing with another event should be avoided, especially if run by a competitor. It is not unknown for rival companies to do this: it irritates the press, reduces the impact, and makes the organisers of the second event look silly.

13

Checklist for effective press relations

In order to maintain an effective press relations programme, the following pointers will be useful.

1. Awareness of impending news possibilities affecting a client or employer is vital, including any developments of their own, so that the press office is prepared and can handle the news, be it good or bad, in the most effective way.
2. Media contact lists must be up to date. Contacts are sometimes absent, so editors (such as city, sport, or whatever) should also receive copies.
3. Stories must be angled for different audiences, whether these are identified by their location, interests, age or sex.
4. Deadlines must be kept in mind.
5. A press conference or briefing should only be called when the story is sufficiently important. Directors or senior managers taking the conference must be briefed and, if possible, rehearsed.
6. Seasonal opportunities can be utilised for some products and services.

7. Draft legislation, the Budget and official statistics all provide opportunities for a client or employer to provide comment. The press will favour those organisations able to provide sound, reasoned comment.
8. Research or other insights can be offered to the media to maintain the relationship when other stories are few and far between.
9. Good photographs are important to illustrate appropriate stories.
10. A photographic library of essential items and people for whom a photograph might be required on demand will improve efficiency.
11. Product or service brochures and other explanatory material should be provided if this will help journalists.
12. Ensuring journalists have the opportunity to sample products or services is essential if a review is needed.
13. Embargoes can be used if the media need time to research a story, or if the news needs to break on a particular day; but otherwise they should be avoided.
14. Advance warning can help to improve coverage in the publications which are of most importance to the story.
15. Quotes should be attributed to someone of sufficient authority and interest to the press, and they should be available for interview whenever possible.
16. Ensure that the story reaches the right publications; and do not simply leave it to the post, especially at Christmas or at other public holidays: use couriers, facsimile machines and the wire service or the Internet!
17. Further opportunities such as background articles or features, interviews or photographic opportunities should always be considered.
18. A contact name must be provided on any material sent to the press, including an out-of-hours telephone number.
19. Clashing with major events or announcements by competitors should be avoided as should busy news days.
20. A photographer should be commissioned for major events, in case the journalists attending are not accompanied by a

press photographer. Only those photographers accustomed to working for the press should be used.

21. Action photographs should be used, which show products at work, using people to provide scale and interest.

22. Racial and gender stereotypes should be avoided when organising photography.

23. Issues which affect an employer or client can provide opportunities for an agreed official reaction.

PART 3

HANDLING THE BROADCAST MEDIA

Michael Bland

14

Why: the importance of broadcast coverage

In the last half-century, television has changed the way we live. It has transformed the way we receive our news and the way our impressions are formed. It has influenced the nature of education ... and helped to kill the art of conversation.

Yet all we do is sit there and watch the thing. Too rarely do we got out there and appear on it ourselves: to *use* it rather than *be used* by it.

With more and more stations on more and more channels putting out more and more programmes, there is room on the screen nowadays for almost anybody with something interesting to say.

Yet thousands of business people, leaders of pressure groups, chambers of commerce and fund-raisers go through life assuming that 'TV is for the pros', that they themselves are doing well if they make half a column in the local paper.

Television is a communications medium which is always searching for entertaining material. Almost anybody can use it to get a message into millions of homes.

For the business person it can be a public relations tool or the death of the business, depending on how it is treated. The same company director who uses other publicity material with the skill of the born salesperson will retreat in terror from a heaven-sent opportunity to display his or her firm or product to vast clientele through a highly credible medium.

Radio, too, is an invaluable medium, with advantages – and one or two rules – of its own, and most of the important messages about television also apply to radio.

With the TV ad you can use both sound and vision to demonstrate the indispensability of your product. You can *show* how fast your cars go, how kids love eating your breakfast cereal, why people use your deodorant spray.

It's so good that there has to be a catch, and there is: money. Television advertising is expensive in the extreme.

Just one minute of prime networked air time can cost as much as £250,000.

Putting it into perspective, you can buy your own studio equipment, send five executives on one-day courses, have ten days of private training for the top person, pay a year's salary for a television press officer and cost a month's working time for the chief executive, all for the price of 15 *seconds* of advertising on a national television programme!

Proactive television

They may come to you because they need an expert – preferably an interesting one – to talk about the subject they are covering.

Or you may be the perceived or potential 'villain' in a negative story. Individual and company reputations can go down the drain before you can say 'Investigative Journalism'. And we've seen others saved by the skilful handling of a crucial interview.

Of course, there will be the odd occasion when you want to keep a low profile and will have good cause to steer clear of the screen. But in the vast majority of cases when people refuse to go on television, it is on a pretext which boils down to: 'They'll ask a lot of awkward questions and make me look a fool.' And that's the heart of it: 'I might be made to look a fool'. It's understandable, but hardly enterprising.

And there are plenty of other excuses. First, there are the horror stories. We've all seen them: an inexperienced spokesperson dying the death of a thousand cuts in front of 20 million people. Someone campaigning for a good cause is made to look a fanatic by skilful editing. A devoted public servant comes over as a bumbling idiot thanks to some loaded questions. And a businessman who has put his prices up to stay alive is turned into a grasping capitalist by a skilful interviewer.

Most of us are uneasy about the alien environment, too. Television studios are so unfamiliar: the lights, the cameras, the trendy people, the clutter, the hassle. Walking into a studio the average first-timer feels like a missionary entering an Amazon head-hunting village.

Nor do we like being made fools of. For verbal bad eggs and visual rotten tomatoes, television is the hottest thing since the village stocks.

And lastly there's that stomach vibrating fear of a large audience. Anyone who has been in a school play or had to make a speech knows how he or she goes all to pieces, when transfixed by hundreds of eyes.

But successful business is all about seizing opportunities, and television presents a glorious opportunity to promote a product, service or cause.

It's the same story whether the news is good or bad. If it's bad – if they are probing into a strike, a fire, a duff product, excess profits – there's no excuse for absence.

If you refuse to respond you will quite certainly be damned in your absence. Without you there to answer back, the presenters, interviewers, union leaders and experts will have a field day.

But by having a go you stand at least a chance of putting some or all of the record straight, and of diverting the viewer's attention to another, more positive, aspect of the business.

Incredibly, however, business people can even run away when it's *good* news. Often a programme which genuinely wants to show a company and its goods in a favourable light has the door slammed in its face by reluctant management who 'don't want a lot of cameras all over the place'.

OK, television is different. We've often seen how people's real personalities are transformed – for better or worse – by being electronically processed and displayed on the screen in two dimensions.

And, whereas a print journalist interviews you for information and subsequently seeks to entertain when he/she writes the copy, a broadcast journalist has to both inform *and* entertain during the interview.

With both print and broadcast media, if you or your message is interesting and entertaining, journalists will be inclined to let you have your say and use what you give them. But when you're not entertaining, when you're pompous, abstract or just plain boring, it starts to go wrong.

The print journalist goes off with your 2000 words of ramblings and looks for a sexy angle for the readers – and thereby 'gets it all wrong'.

And the television interviewer hears the producer's voice in the earpiece saying, 'God, this is boring, liven it up!' So he shoves a pointed stick through the bars and pokes you into 'performing', ie starts to ask some nasty questions and generally duff you up for the entertainment of the viewers.

It helps to understand why they need to do this. Despite their protestations to the contrary, the media are driven by a 'commercial imperative'. If they don't constantly attract people to watch, listen and read then they will cease to exist. Very quickly. TV producers and interviewers have a constant neurosis that if the viewers find their programme less interesting than the others they will switch over and not come back. Then the viewing figures drop ... and the TV people are out of a job.

Thus the driving force behind a TV interview – *your* interview – is a couch potato with a zapper and a very short attention span. A depressing thought!

So, except for a small minority of malicious or biased programmes, all that the programme makers want from your interview is 'colour'. And if you don't give them colour *your* way they will get it from you *their* way. And you won't like it.

Now let's look at how to provide it *your* way.

15

How: preparation and briefing

Everyone nods in agreement when told that thorough preparation is essential. Yet almost every disaster on TV is caused by a lack of preparation.

You can – and must – do a great deal to prepare yourself to communicate at your best and avoid being tripped up. Many interviewees who complain of being misrepresented have in fact been guilty of going into the studio with a blind (and seriously misguided) faith that the questions will enable them to communicate their messages.

Asking the questions

The prospective interviewee needs to know the following about the programme they are to appear on:

- What is the programme about?
- Why have they picked on this particular interviewee?
- What is their source of information? If it is a press cutting, read it beforehand.

- What do they know already?
- What do they want to learn?
- In what context will the contribution be used?
- How long will the contribution be?
- Is it to be live or recorded? If recorded, how much of the interview will actually be used in the final programme?
- Will they be using any film or props?
- Who else is going on the programme (such as a competitor or customer)?
- An idea of the questions would also be helpful.

Consideration needs to be given to the following:

- The exact form of the questions is usually only decided at the last minute, and if the interviewer finds an interesting line of discussion during the programme, it is their job to probe further and forget the original questions.
- The interviewer should have an idea of the sort of questions they want to ask. Television interviewers are professionals. So are their research teams, and they will be already thinking about their line of questioning.
- The line of questioning will give a guide to how the interview will run. If possible, an agreement on the first subject to be covered will help the interview off to a smooth start.
- 'Playing it by ear' will result in a poor performance. At least an hour of preparation is ideal. If the request is for an immediate response, a few minutes clarifying the message will pay dividends.
- The purpose of appearing on television is to deliver a planned message, not what the interviewer wants them to say.

Skeleton plan

Say, for example, you are a vegetarian and you have an opportunity to encourage a few million others to become vegetarian too. Your knowledge of the subject is vast. There is a wealth of things that the simple carnivore should be taught – economical vegetarian diets, suffering of animals, cholesterol, flavour and thousands of other things.

But now the requirement is to condense all this knowledge into a basic message. At best the speaker will get three points over. And in any case, the viewers won't remember more than two or three points. These might be:

1. Vegetables are better and cheaper than meat.
2. Meat is high in cholesterol.
3. There are not enough animals to go round.

These points should be the basis of everything said during the interview. Whatever the questions, whatever the angle, these points should be stressed.

At this point subsections can be added: for example, point 1 above can be split up:

1. Vegetables are better and cheaper than meat:

    (a) vegetables are half the cost of meat;
    (b) vegetables contain all the protein and nutrients you need;
    (c) vegetables are healthier because they contain roughage; and
    (d) you can grow them in your own garden.

There should be a maximum of three main points, each supported by some subpoints. That skeleton could get the main points over in a couple of minutes.

Brevity

Years of thinking and millions of words and figures have gone into brief phrases like: 'What's good for General Motors is good for America'; 'There is no such thing as a free lunch'; and 'From each according to his ability, to each according to his needs.' This principle of brevity should be kept in mind when communicating something in a short space of time. On television there is very little time is offered, so the punchline must come at the beginning.

Simplicity

The television audience is probably ironing, eating, reading, arguing, putting the kids to bed or thinking of changing channels. Even when the television has their undivided attention they are mentally relaxed and only concentrating at half power. Thus the message must be very simple.

Repetition

It is better to say the same thing several times than to say several things once. Words and sentences should be short so that everyone knows what is being said. For example the CBI succeeded with a campaign against the National Insurance surcharge largely by calling it 'the jobs tax'.

Impact

Which of the following statements has more impact?

● Animal fats are bad for you and can be fatal.
● A friend of mine died from eating animal fats.

The latter actually gives a picture of someone dying from indulging in non-vegetarian activities.
Which of these would viewers relate to more?

● The new factory will improve local employment.
● Albert Jones bought his friends a drink today for the first time in three years; that's how long he was out of work before this factory was built.

The first one may be shorter, yet it has less impact than the second. People love stories. Possibly the greatest communicator of all time was Jesus Christ. His philosophy is still grasped by hundreds of millions of people in all languages, 2000 years after his death, partly because he said it all in stories. For example, if he had just told people to have a care for those they did not like, the homily would have been forgotten by morning. So he told them about a Samaritan who took pity on a mugging victim. The message still gets through today.

For instance, the fact that vegetables are half the cost of meat can be illustrated with a story such as: 'half a pound of steak costs a fortune. Baked potatoes topped with cheese and celery for all the family costs half what that steak cost.'

Familiarity

Another effective way of communicating is to ring a bell in the other person's mind with something with which he or she is already familiar. Again, Christ was the master at this. How hard is it for a sinner to get into heaven? As hard as it is for a camel to go through the eye of a needle. What better description of a false prophet than a 'ravening wolf dressed as a sheep'?

In talking about a new factory, describing it as 'about the size of 8000 square metres' is difficult to grasp. Could it be put into everyday terms? 'About the size of two football fields' is much more readily understood. Does a reservoir contain 123,455,200 gallons of water or does it hold three weeks' supply for the town? Does a refinery have an unpleasant aroma of sulphur dioxide or does it smell like bad eggs?

Relevance: the 'So what?' test

Finally, go back through everything you intend to say and subject it to the 'So what?' test. It may be terribly important to you ... but what about the viewer? If it isn't relevant to him or her, why are you saying it?

Learn the brief

So far so good. The first part of the preparation time has been spent thinking out:

- why you are going on the programme
- what is to be said and
- how to say it.

The interviewee must know the brief so well that a relevant message springs to mind when asked a relevant question. There is a big difference between knowing the message and actually saying it. The interviewee should practise saying the key messages aloud. Be clear about the message, then prepare responses to certain potential questions.

What questions are likely to be asked?

Journalists are only human and there is a finite number of questions they can ask about anything. A brainstorming session with colleagues will probably give rise to most possible angles. Remember the basic questions: Who? What? When? Where? How? Why?

If the programme is a positive one (eg local news, diary or chat show) most of the questions will be aimed at extracting the good news. Others, especially investigative programmes, will be looking for the negatives.

Likely questions should be listed so that the interviewee is not thrown by the unexpected during the interview. But remember that you aren't going to *answer* the questions – you are going to *use* them to put your points across.

Watching different programmes and their different approaches is valid preparation, as is familiarising yourself with the different interviewers. By watching television in an analytical, questioning frame of mind, you can work out for yourself what makes a good or bad interview. When watching a television interview, the following questions can be asked:

- How did he or she get on that programme?
- Is he or she doing a good job?
- What are the programme-makers looking for?
- Could I get on that programme?
- How would I set about it?

Preparing for the interview

Before the interview

The moments before a TV interview can be quite nerve-racking.

An ENG (electronic news-gathering) unit – usually a reporter and cameraman plus a single camera, but often just one person both interviewing and operating the camera – can be disconcerting. But a studio can be even more terrifying with its bright lights, banks of cameras, cables, technicians and many other personnel. The pre-interview period can be used like the warm-up.

Nerves

People worry too much about controlling nerves. If the speaker is genuinely paralysed by them, an acting school can give advice on how to learn a technique such as the 'squeeze' which inhibits the flow of adrenaline. However, adrenaline can help to produce a good performance.

Some tips to help with nerves:

- Avoid alcohol.
- Avoid nervous, unstructured conversation with anyone who is at hand. Nothing is 'off the record'.
- Ask questions, such as: How much do they know about the subject? How long will the interview run? How much of it are they likely to broadcast? What do they want to ask? Who else are they talking to?

Rehearse

This is the time to rehearse the messages, so that they are in the front of your mind.

Think positive

Psychologically the interviewer has just one major advantage: the fact that he or she is asking the questions. Treat each question not as a *threat* but as an *opportunity* to get one of the key messages across.

Bridging from the questions

By treating the questions as opportunities you will soon get the hang of 'bridging' from what they have asked to what you want to say. It works like this: say one of your messages is that you've just reduced your golf handicap and you want to get this across whatever the question:

Q.   Is it true that cholesterol is bad for you?

A.   In small amounts, it's probably actually *good* for you – but there's a lot of evidence that if you have too much it can *kill* you. But the negative effects will also depend on your lifestyle, as the right kind of exercise helps to burn it off before it does any damage. My own recipe is golf. By playing twice a week I manage to keep my cholesterol level down and reduce my handicap.

This has (a) answered the question; (b) developed into a 'bridging theme' and (c) moved on to the message. In this case the bridging theme was 'exercise', which was relevant to both cholesterol and golf. It comes easily with practice.

Many if not most of the questions will enable a response with the prepared message as they will be immediately directly relevant. If the first question is: 'What's the best way to burn off cholesterol?', golf can be introduced without bridging.

The bar-room interview

Imagine yourself not in a TV studio but in a favourite pub, club or wine bar, chatting with a stranger who starts to ask a few questions about work, product, or cause.

Natural communication involves instinctively leaning forward, looking the questioner in the eye, modulating your voice, using simple language, practical examples and anecdotes, and speaking with enthusiasm and conviction.

Dress and looks

A popular myth has grown up that looks are the most important aspect of a television appearance. This is nonsense. Look at TV for yourself. Who are the people who really jump out of the screen and grab attention? The highly groomed politicians and business leaders? No – it is those who have something interesting to say and who say it with colour and zest.

Obviously, though, loud or scruffy clothes or a sloppy

manner or nervous swivelling and fidgeting will detract from the message. The main thing is that the interviewee feels comfortable in what they are wearing, but there a few technicalities to bear in mind:

- Stripes or checks, particularly narrow ones have a stroboscopic effect and appear to be moving.
- Equally disconcerting is flashing jewellery, tie-pins, etc.
- Clashing or really loud colours (especially red, which 'bleeds' at the edges) should be avoided.
- Almost black and off-white are OK (a bit drab, perhaps) but straight black and white sends colour cameras bananas.
- Interviewees need to check just before going on to avoid stray hair, slipped tie knots and smudged mascara.

Example of a final brief

XTV Look Round
Vegetarian interview
Interviewer: Cliff Hanger

1. Vegetables better and cheaper:
   - half the price of meat
   - all protein requirements
   - healthier – roughage (example of a fit vegetarian)
   - grow them in own garden (fun!).

2. Why meat is bad:
   - cholesterol (dead friend)
   - impurities (fertiliser poisons)
   - bad for teeth.

3. Ecological:
   - increasing human population (500 new humans born during this interview)
   - decreasing animals
   - suffering:
     - rearing conditions (describe calf in pen)
     - slaughtering conditions (describe slaughterhouse).

Checklist

PREPARATION

1. Decide whether to do it or not:

   - who is doing the interview?
   - when?
   - where?
   - how long will it last?

2. Decide:

   - is someone available?
   - is it worth doing?

3. If so ask:

   - why are they doing this programme?
   - why pick on this organisation?
   - what is the context?
   - will it be live or recorded?
   - any films or props?
   - who else will be on the programme?
   - what questions will they ask?

4. Prepare – at least an hour

   - Plan the message:
     - maximum three points (distil them; time is short) supported by some sub-points
   - learn the brief.

5. Anticipate the angle and likely questions.

16

How: winning the interview

Editors, producers, directors, floor managers, researchers, cameramen, secretaries, not to mention their deputies and assistants are all involved in making a programme. It is fairly safe to assume that the person making the most noise between takes is the producer, while the one making all the noise during takes is the director.

Forget the cameras and look at the interviewer. Looking into the camera during an interview appears contrived, and there is a chance of looking into the wrong camera. A red light on top of the camera lights up when it is on, but even experienced newscasters often play Russian roulette between the red lights. There is no way of knowing when the director will order a different camera to cut in.

Many people use notes or reports as security blankets, arriving at the studio with a great pile of them only to be reduced to a nervous wreck when they are asked not to take them into the studio. A notepad on the knee can actually give quite a professional look, especially if it conveys the impression of being armed with plenty of facts and figures. The great big golden rule is not to read from them. If the camera catches someone peering at their notes in a frantic search for the answer to the last question, then they will not seem credible to the viewer any more.

A poor interview

Suddenly, it is all about to happen for real. A voice calls out '30 seconds'. Then the interviewer speaks, and the cameras are recording. Let us now create a victim and look at a duff interview. The characters and every aspect of the script are borrowed from what happens in real life – from different interviews at different times, in different words. Though fictional, the interview is certainly not impossible. And a highly controversial subject has been chosen to show how even the indefensible can be defended by a skilful interviewee.

We have a typical interviewee – a businessman – and a typical interviewer. A businessman has been selected as one of the vast group of people who are likely to be asked to do an interview, yet who has the least experience in television techniques. But the things we are about to see – the questions, the tricks, the pitfalls, the missed opportunities – apply to everyone.

The story so far

Oscar Winner is chief executive of Basket Eggs, a big poultry and egg producer. The company has announced plans to build a plant at Foxtooth, a town of 100,000 inhabitants. It will be one of the biggest companies in the region, and the local TV station has brought Winner in to be interviewed on the evening current affairs programme.

The interviewer, Susan Sharp, is a seasoned pro. In real life she is a nice woman, with a husband and four children. She feeds the ducks on a Sunday afternoon. But she is a bit cynical about businessmen and has one fault: if she thinks someone is a baddie, or is trying to pull a fast one she goes in for the kill. She has told Winner about her line of questioning, but has been pretty vague, 'What will the factory do?', 'How much will it cost?', 'Any particular problems?' etc.

Winner, for his part, is completely confident about the interview. There is nothing he does not know about chickens; he is a good after-dinner speaker; and his wife thinks he is handsome. He is so calm about it, in fact, that he got in a quick nine holes at the local golf course before going to the studios.

It is 6.30pm, and the interview is going out live. Sharp launches into her introduction. The script is set out below. Most of the studio directions are omitted for simplicity, and the numbers are inserted for reference when we analyse the interview afterwards. Read it through in one go before going back through the numbers.

SHARP: Our next guest on the programme is someone who has a lot to answer for. He's Oscar Winner [*cut to Winner sitting back* (1) *smiling*] who's to build a poultry plant on the outskirts of Foxtooth. The type of plant planned is to be like the one in this film [*film, 45 seconds, showing rearing of chicks and battery conditions, some birds dying, most losing feathers etc* (2)]. Mr Winner, why are you bringing this kind of thing to Foxtooth?

WINNER: (3) Well, it's a logical decision. The company is expanding and Foxtooth is an ideal location for a new poultry plant. In fact ...

SHARP: (4) But we've just seen how senseless suffering is caused to countless thousands of chickens. Why not buy a field here and let them fly around a bit?

WINNER: (5) Ah, that simply wouldn't be economical, Susan (6). On a free-range basis you need a square-footage-to-bird ratio of 14.7:1 on grade A feed, and more on lower quality grain (7).

SHARP: Are you saying that you practically torture helpless birds, simply because it's more profitable that way?

WINNER: Well, it's hardly torture (8). I'm just saying that all the people watching this programme ... (9).

SHARP: We all know, though, that your method produces lower-quality eggs (4). In the film they showed a waste-burning unit: are you going to bring one of those here?

WINNER: (5) Oh yes. That's standard equipment in this sort of plant.

SHARP: But that chimney in the film was belching filthy black smoke over the neighbourhood. Now you're telling us that we're to have a factory chimney polluting the atmosphere (10).

WINNER: Well (11), I should like to reassure the viewers that the chimney will only produce about 120,000 cubic feet of waste smoke per hour [*pause*]. Besides, er ... (13) [*pause*] this sort of production requires a certain amount of recycling and waste-burning and so on (14).

SHARP: All the same, 120,000 cubic feet sounds like an awful lot of black smoke for a small town like Foxtooth. Tell me, Mr Winner, how long is the plant going to take to build?

WINNER: Just under a year, we hope, though the first eggs should be in production on a limited scale within nine months. We've got a really good firm on the job, and once it's finished it'll be the most modern plant of its kind.

SHARP: Who's building the plant for you then?

WINNER: I ... (15) Why do you want to know? (16)

SHARP: It would be interesting to know if it's a local firm. The construction industry round here has been going through a rough patch lately, hasn't it?

WINNER: Has it? (17) I must admit I'm not using a local firm ...

SHARP: Why not?

WINNER: Well, quite simply because we've chosen Stackbricks to do the job.

SHARP: Why Stackbricks, though?

WINNER: Well ... I mean ... [*angrily*] (18) look, why are you asking me all this stuff about the builders? You're making me sound as though I've been bribed or something! (19)

SHARP: [*coolly*] OK, so it's a year from now and you've built the factory. What benefit are we going to get out of it?

WINNER: Well, I think (20) the great advantage of the Winner system is that you get more eggs for less money. Everything is automatic so we can cut costs and provide a cheaper egg by the thousand.

SHARP: I see. Do you have enough eggs for export, then?

WINNER: Oh yes! We even sell frozen eggs to the People's Republic of China!

SHARP: I'm glad to hear it. That's Mr Oscar Winner, who's going to build a plant here to send eggs to China. What the people of Foxtooth will do for eggs is anybody's guess (21) [*cut*].

That interview took just over two minutes. In that time our friend Mr Winner put his foot in it at least 21 times. Interviewers are not always as tough as Sharp, and interviewees not always as dumb as Winner. But many of those 21 points will crop up even in the kindest interview. Let us go back over the interview, point by point, and see why Mr Winner did not make it. All the points are important, but five are golden rules (numbers 4, 5, 8, 16 and 20).

1. Look alert

It is terribly tempting to try to relax in a studio chair. This can make someone look too contented – if not a complete slob. It is especially true if the opening gambit is an attack: the camera catches them sitting back, smiling smugly, and the viewer already wants to see the interviewer wipe that silly smile right off their face.

2. Any surprises?

If they are using a film the interviewee should insist on seeing it first. The same applies to surprise studio guests and any other gimmicks.

3. Shout 'unfair'

If they say it is impossible, or say there is no file and then spring it anyway, the viewer must know right away that the interviewee has not seen it.

4. Do not let the interviewer butt in

In normal conversation people tend to stop when someone butts in. On television the reverse applies. If the interviewer cuts in the interviewee should raise their voice – slightly but firmly – and finish what they were saying. Do not confuse making a point with waffle. Finish the point then shut up. Twenty seconds is adequate – unless it is something that is both important and interesting (eg a colourful anecdote).

5. Refute incorrect statements

What kind of a question was that? Here Sharp is using a derogatory statement followed by a different question. It is a favourite trick.

6. No names

It is a small point, but do not forget that ultimately you are talking to the viewer. Be especially careful of first names. They can make the interview sound a bit contrived or 'pally'.

7. No jargon

That spiel about the 14.7:1 ratio may look ludicrous, but it happens all the time. People are so used to the gobbledegook of their everyday jobs that they forget the viewer cannot understand a word of it. Remember instead the advice in Chapter 15 about using simple analogies. (For example: a space expert in a recent interview explained the nature and dimensions of a Soyuz space station: 'It fits together like a child's construction set. With the latest addition it's now about the size of a domestic garage.')

8. Do not defend

Somehow on television it is as bad as an admission of guilt. She used the word 'torture': now Winner used the same word again which is just what she wanted. Far from being on the defensive in a television interview, use the offensive – in the nicest possible way!

9. There is only one viewer

He or she is an individual, not 'one' or the 'audience' or the 'viewer'. By speaking to him or her through the interviewer it should not be necessary to refer to them as anyone in particular – just 'you'.

10. Don't let them misinterpret

An interviewer will often paraphrase the message. It is usually done with good intentions to achieve simplicity. But if it is done to the detriment of the speaker, they should put it straight at once.

11. 'Well ...'

It is human nature to start with a 'Well ...' It does not do any harm in small doses, but that is the third time Winner has started with 'Well' in five questions. He is losing impact.

12. The calculated pause

The pregnant pause is a device much loved of psychologists and police interrogators. Silence is awkward when in close proximity to a stranger and people feel obliged to fill it. A clever interviewer may sometimes just sit there looking and waiting for the interviewee to say something they may later regret. The interviewer is only too conscious that if the interview is filled with long pauses she will be chewed out by the producer for a boring piece. The onus is on her to keep things flowing. If she clams up suddenly and deliberately, having got over a key point the interviewee should shut up and wait for the interviewer to crack first.

13. 'Er, um ...'

It is worth some practice in everyday speech. The more 'um' and 'er' and 'ah', the less certain someone sounds about the facts.

14. 'And so on and so forth and the like ...'

Meaningless. List your items and quit while you're ahead.

15. He who hesitates

A brief pause for thought is OK, as is meeting a deliberate pregnant pause with silence. But in the wrong circumstances a long pause for thought can look dishonest. And it is also important to keep the interview lively and moving at a good pace.

Incidentally, quite a good breathing-space technique is to ask the interviewer to repeat the question (though obviously it would look ridiculous after a simple question like the one about the builders). In fact in this particular case Sharp's question is a sidetrack and right now Winner should not be answering the question at all.

16. Do not be sidetracked

Interviewers are always looking for a dark alleyway with a corpse at the end of it. (This is one reason for not relying too much on prepared questions and answers.) A good interviewer can sniff trouble a mile away at the end of a sidetrack. The question of who is building the plant is of immense local interest, though you can see that Sharp had not thought of it – she got the lead accidentally from Winner ('We've got a really good firm on the job ...').

17. Know your ground

It should go without saying. Interviewers are often backed up by research teams who ply them with facts and figures. Do not make it worse with a dumb retort like 'Has it?'

18. Stay cool

Never get angry. Be firm but polite.

19. Do not volunteer things

Winner has just done exactly what Sharp wanted him to do. Sharp knew she would be in hot water if she made any allegations of corruption, so, she has let Winner imply the allegations himself.

20. Be positive

Terms like 'I think', 'It seems that', 'I believe' reduce a firm statement of fact to a personal view. Be assertive. Material should be presented as fact, not opinion.

21. The last word

Another favourite. Under the guise of 'winding up', the interviewer delivers the *coup-de-grâce* while the interviewee sits there open-mouthed and the clock ticks to zero. Do not let them get away with it. Register disagreement at once or silence could be mistaken for acceptance.

The key points

Winner's first and biggest mistake has been saved till now. He went in cold, without a brief. He failed to hammer any key points home – because he did not have any key points to hammer home in the first place. He made the cardinal error of playing the interview by ear because he thought he had all the answers in his head.

Go over Winner's interview and look for the main points he should have got over. He wants to make it clear that Basket Eggs is good news. What are the positive points?

1. For a start, it must be demonstrable that eggs are beneficial or presumably one would not eat them. This is a great time for Winner to be selling his product and to make the viewer want to go out and buy a dozen.

2. A major investment in a plant can be shown to be a benefit to the community. Basket Eggs is sure to provide jobs, to add to the income from rates and to boost local trade.
3. Mass production should make for cheaper eggs: that is good news for the shopper.

Of course, there are other points – those valuable exports to China, for example. But Winner should not concentrate on more than two or three points. The viewer simply cannot absorb any more. Other points can be slipped in if there is time. It is worth noting, from these three points alone, how quickly Sharp's irresistible nasties could be spotted in advance. For example, there are plenty of experts who say eggs are bad for people; there is the fact that a new plant will destroy some piece of greenery; and what about those poor old hens?

In any case Winner should have come to terms long ago with the negative aspects of his business. It would be wrong to pretend that everything is perfect in business, and Winner's line of work is full of warts which it would be both immoral and impractical to try to hide. His job here is to highlight the positive points and play down the negative ones.

A good interview: getting the message across

It is incredibly simple: there is not a question in the world that cannot be turned to an advantage. Every question is nothing more than a peg to hang a case on. There are varying degrees. Some questions are 'gifts'. Most questions, however, require some kind of answer before getting on to one's own material. Only as a very last resort should a question be ignored completely.

Let us say, for example, that Sharp throws in a question about production: 'Just how many eggs a day will your plant produce?' A fair enough question. But Winner's first key point had nothing to do with the number of eggs: it was to tell the viewer that eggs are good for you and you should eat more. He knows his plant will produce 50,000 eggs a day: now all he has to do is to add a bit: 'Fifty thousand. That's 50,000 meals. One egg alone has enough protein and vitamins to keep you going for half a day.'

Well, Susan Sharp is a seasoned pro and knows propaganda when she sees it, so she quickly changes tack: 'According to some experts, eggs can cause heart failure – is this what you're advocating?' But Winner has not finished selling his eggs. It would be a mistake to skip the heart-failure problem altogether so he uses the question: 'Taken to excess, anything causes heart failure. But a couple of eggs a day are really good for you – and they're so versatile. They're delicious boiled, fried, scrambled and in omelettes.'

At the same time, though, many interviewers are getting wise to these evasion techniques. Let us say Sharp asks Winner how much profit he made last year. Winner knows he made a packet. And he knows Sharp knows it. This is a case for a 'perspective' answer, rather than evasion:

- 'Last year was an exceptionally good one, but let's get it in perspective. We made £30 million, but eggs are a highly risky business and with all the money we're putting into the Foxtooth plant we'll need all the cash we can get.'
- 'It works out at a tenth of a penny per egg.'
- 'At first sight it looks a lot – £50 million pre-tax in fact – but don't forget £20 million of that goes straight to the Government to provide schools, defence and welfare ...'

Sharp is only waiting for the figure. The moment Winner says £30 or £50 million, she will leap in with: '*£30 million*! Here you are making a killing while ...' Do not let her get away with it. Keep talking and insist on making the point.

Now it is time to apply the lessons to Winner's first interview. The story is the same. The people are the same, and to demonstrate how Winner should have dealt with each question, the questions are the same:

SHARP: Our next guest on the programme is someone who has a lot to answer for. He's Oscar Winner [*cut to Winner, sitting up, intent and alert*] who's to build a poultry plant on the outskirts of Foxtooth. The type of plant planned is to be like the one in this film [*film, 45 seconds, showing rearing of chicks and battery conditions, some birds dying, most losing feathers, etc*]. Mr Winner, why are you bringing this kind of thing to Foxtooth?

WINNER: (1) If you'd shown me the film before the programme I could have told you how out of date it was. It completely failed to show the immense improvement in the standards of egg production in the last few years. (2) The Foxtooth plant ...

SHARP: But we've just seen ...

WINNER: (3) [*more firmly*] The Foxtooth plant will give a vital boost to what is probably the most important area of food production today (4).

SHARP: But we've just seen how senseless suffering is caused to countless thousands of chickens. Why not buy a field here and let them fly around a bit?

WINNER: If you'd shown film of a field of chickens you'd have seen why (5). Next time you see a flock of free-range chickens, just watch them for a while. Their life is hell. You'll see that a few strong birds peck the others into a state where they're so miserable that they lay far less eggs than their protected sisters in a battery plant (6).

SHARP: Are you saying that you practically torture helpless birds, simply because it's more profitable that way?

WINNER: (7) All the evidence points to the fact that our hens have a safer and longer life and lay more eggs (8). We can check them the whole time so we know that every egg which leaves our plant is good and wholesome.

SHARP: We all know, though, that your method produces lower-quality eggs. In the film they showed a waste-burning unit: are you going to bring one of those here?

WINNER: (9) Listen, our eggs have been tested side by side with free-range eggs and they are every bit as good. Do you realise that there are more protein and nutrients in one single egg than in any other foodstuff at the price? (10)

SHARP: What about this waste-burning unit?

WINNER: Either you have a pile of chicken feathers a mile high or you process them (11). As a matter of fact our process has a number of useful side products – manure, chicken paste, offal (12).

SHARP: But that chimney in the film was belching filthy black smoke over the neighbourhood. Now you're telling us that we're to have a factory chimney polluting the atmosphere.

WINNER: I'm telling you the exact opposite. It will produce no more smoke than half a dozen domestic chimneys (13) – and only occasionally at that.

SHARP: Tell me, Mr Winner, how long is the plant going to take to build?

WINNER: The sooner the better as far as everyone's concerned! When this plant is in production it'll mean 200 new jobs for Foxtooth (14). It's the biggest industrial investment in this region for years.

SHARP: Who's building the plant for you then?

WINNER: (15) It's important first to look at the scope of the project. These new buildings will be the most up to date, safe and efficient in the world. We're investing a fortune to produce the best eggs at the lowest price.

SHARP: But it would be interesting to know if it's a local firm. The construction industry round here has been going through a rough patch lately, hasn't it?

WINNER: (16) It has everywhere, I'm afraid, and of course we looked at the local building firms when we tendered. In this case we chose Stackbricks because of their experience of building this sort of plant. Next time you're in the Ducktown

region take a look at the big, modern egg farm they built there
... (17)

SHARP: OK, so it's a year from now and you've built the
factory. What benefit are we going to get out of it? (18)

WINNER: (19) The biggest single benefit is that you'll get
more eggs for less money. Everything is automatic so we can cut
costs and give you a cheaper egg.

SHARP: I see. Do you have enough eggs for export, then?

WINNER: Oh yes! We even sell frozen eggs to the People's
Republic of China.

SHARP: I'm glad to hear it. That's Mr Oscar Winner, who says
he's going to build a plant here to send eggs to China. Meanwhile,
I wonder what the people of Foxtooth will do for eggs.

WINNER: (20) They come first, of course ... [cut].

That's more like it

There is no such thing as a perfect interview, but this time
Winner made a good showing by applying some elementary
techniques. With the same story and basically the same
questions he got his key points over and dealt firmly with the
nasty questions. What's more Sharp and her bosses will be
pleased with this more lively and informative interview, so the
odds have improved on Winner being invited back for another
go – when the factory opens, for example.

It is worth a look back over the interview to examine the ways
Winner improved. This time he scored 20 times. We will just run
over the inserted numbers and see what lessons he learnt:

1. He is making it clear to the viewer, right from the start,
    that he has not been given a chance to see the film. Not
    only does this stop him making a fool of himself, but it also
    encourages the viewer to side with Winner over this unfair
    treatment.
2. Then he immediately uses the unseen film as a bridge to
    stress the improvements in egg production.

3. No nonsense. He had not finished speaking so he beat Sharp at her own game and cut in. Note that he does so firmly rather than loudly.

4. At the start of the interview, Winner has now got two points in already. He has used the 'improvements' bit as a peg for reminding the viewer that eggs are an important food product.

5. In the first interview he was on the defensive over this 'suffering' accusation. This time he attacks by comparing it with the apparently greater suffering of free-range chickens.

6. Now he is telling a story – painting a picture for the viewer of a lot of chickens giving each other a rough time.

7. Sharp will not give in on his 'suffering' angle. So Winner uses it to reiterate his view that his chickens are happier.

8. He also realises, though, that Sharp is starting to sidetrack him with this 'suffering' angle. So, before Sharp can get started again, Winner bangs in another key point on the back of his 'happy hens' argument. He is starting to make the viewer feel like eating an egg.

9. This is the nearest he gets to showing anger. Underneath he is furious at Sharp's sniping, but that 'listen …' is firm not angry, and he is really telling the viewer: 'listen to me, not her.'

10. Again he uses the moment to sell a few more eggs.

11. It does not take much imagination to convert a simple reassurance about a waste-burning unit into an image in the viewer's mind of a pile of chicken feathers a mile high. Yet it doubles the impact.

12. 'And while we're on the subject of the waste-burner', Winner says in effect: 'Look at all the goodies you are going to get out of my factory.' His plug for chicken paste does not really have much to do with the waste-burner, but it only takes a few words to link the two.

13. Here is a good example of an analogy. Gone are the 120,000 cubic feet and in their place are half a dozen domestic chimneys – which the viewer can picture at once.

14. It has taken a couple of minutes for Winner to have a chance to get this key point in, but he is not going to let it go. Again, he used the question as a bridge. If he merely answers the question 'How long is it going to take to build?', he will never demonstrate the boost he is giving to employment in the region. The technique is essential and simple, but it requires constant practice.

15. Winner smells obvious trouble in the question about the builders. It can only be trouble as there is no other reason for asking a dumb question like that. So he sidesteps the question, if a little crudely, and gets on with another plug. But this time it does not work. It is a reasonable attempt to evade the question, and he has gained some thinking time, but he realises that Sharp is not going to let this one go in a hurry.

16. So this time he says who the builders are, but quickly explains, honestly and rationally, the reason for the choice. Note his initial response: in fact he does not know any more about the local construction scene than he did in the first interview, but 'It has everywhere, I'm afraid' shows much more apparent understanding and sympathy than 'Has it?'

17. Now he is painting a picture for the viewer again and starting, in effect, to describe what his new plant will look like.

18. Sharp has interrupted again, but she also happens to be changing the subject, which is just what Winner wants. So this time he lets her.

19. Do not look a gift horse in the mouth! If a straight answer gets the key message over, then give a straight answer.

20. It is not much of a rejoinder but he has got to be quick. At least he points out that Foxtooth will get its eggs, and he spoils Sharp's snide little wind-up.

Just by using a few rules, a few techniques, all of them very simple, yet with a bit of preparation and practice, the same person achieves a vast improvement. One thing which does not show in a script is sincerity. This time round Winner has scored several points, but it is important to avoid being smug or snide when winning. It can be tempting to sit back with a satisfied smile, but this must be avoided at all costs.

Once the interview has been wound up the interviewee should remain sitting, looking at the interviewer, until someone tells them it is over.

Checklist

PREPARATION

1. Let them do all the fussing:
    * show you to your seat
    * fix microphone, etc
    * ask them questions.

2. Last check on clothing:
    * stray hair
    * straighten tie, shirt, etc
    * pull down coat at back.

3. Voice test – same value as in the interview.

APPEARANCE AND MANNER

1. Sit up.

2. Look at interviewer throughout

3. Speak clearly and distinctly.

4. Use hands, and do not be afraid of mannerisms, but avoid fussy or nervous movements.

5. Have notes, but do not read from them.

6. Be sincere and enthusiastic throughout.

HANDLING THE INTERVIEW

Platinum rule

> Get the key points to the viewer, regardless of the questions and other distractions.

Golden rules

1. Do not let the interviewer butt in without a fight.
2. Refute any incorrect statements.
3. Stay off the defensive.
4. Do not get sidetracked.
5. Be positive.

Silver rules

1. Look alert.
2. Try to anticipate surprises.
3. Let the viewer know about surprises.
4. Do not address the interviewer by name.
5. If the interviewer rephrases your statements, make sure he or she has got them right.
6. Do not use jargon.
7. Remember there is only one viewer.
8. Avoid too many 'wells . . .'.
9. Do not fill embarrassing silences. That is the interviewer's job.
10. Stay off the 'ums' and 'ers'.
11. Do not tail off with 'and so on', 'and so forth'.
12. Only hesitate if it is deliberate.
13. Know the facts.
14. Do not get angry.
15. Do not volunteer irrelevant information.
16. Watch for the interviewer getting in a harmful last word.

17

Fine tuning: handling different interviews

We have already looked at how programmes can vary. Most are just looking for some colour and will only become hostile if they do not get it.

But there are also one or two consumer and investigative programmes for which, on the business side of the fence, the organisations are presumed guilty before the start and some unsavoury techniques are employed to prove it.

All programmes should be treated with caution; and thorough preparation should be made. There are also some different types of interview and it is worth taking a brief look at the differences:

Live

Relatively few interviews are live – but they should be welcomed. The knowledge that it is for real can enhance a performance. It also guarantees that nothing can be lost or misinterpreted in subsequent editing.

Recorded

Most interviews are recorded – but treat them just as though they were live. The first take is almost always the best. (This is also why the device of countering a pause with a pause still works on recorded interviews – the pressure on the interviewer is almost as strong as in a live one.) However, if the interviewee mucks it up in the first take, they can stop and ask them to do it again – especially if they do something offside, such as introduce new evidence.

Panel

This is where there is more than one person being interviewed – sometimes a whole studio audience. Obviously, the more interviewees the less messages will come across from each. The most important message must be crystal clear and in the front of your mind.

By being more interesting and colourful than the rest and not being afraid to step in if the occasion warrants, individuals can steer the odds in their favour. The director is also looking for movement so a judicious leaning forward or the pointing of a pen or finger can help.

Down-the-line

This is where an interviewee is in a studio in town A and is being interviewed by someone in town B. At first it can be very distracting as there is no one to talk with – just a disembodied voice and the self-consciousness of talking into a camera.

The best tip for a down-the-line interview, apart from getting used to it with practice, is to remember that talking via a microphone and a speaker with someone unseen is done everyday on a telephone!

Down-the-line and single operator ENG (ie one person both

interviewing and holding the camera) interviews are the only times that the interviewee may have to look into the camera.

On site

The advice so far has dealt with a studio interview but programme-makers will often come to an organisation with a camera. The techniques are just the same but it can feel different in some respects.

People usually feel more at ease on their own territory and perform a little better. This is particularly true if you are standing up. We usually come over more positively when standing hence the advice to sit *up* in a seated interview. We also tend to perform better out of doors than in. But watch out for the position of the camera. They will usually be looking for the most attractive or relevant backdrop but it is not unknown for the 'villains' to position someone carefully in front of the factory's only chimney when it is belching black smoke, or beside a drum of chemicals with a skull and crossbones on it.

Afterwards they will often do things like 'noddies' (getting the interviewee and/or the interviewer to sit there showing silent interest in the other person's comments and questions) or re-filming the interviewer asking the questions. These are not tricks. They are simply devices to give them 'cutaway' footage to avoid 'jump cuts' during editing.

Doorstep

In exceptional (usually controversial) circumstances they may 'doorstep' someone by appearing from nowhere and trying to throw them into an instant interview. Do not be drawn into it.

But you also cannot afford just to slam the door or run away as they will capture this on film and show it as evidence of 'guilt'. The answer is a half-way house: stating at once that you are prepared to talk – and immediately giving a good reason why it cannot be done just now (going to an urgent meeting, etc).

Or if you are outside your home or offices, they could be invited in, so that they have to dismantle the camera and set it up again – during which time some useful preparation can be done.

Programme-makers' own official guidelines tell them that they cannot doorstep unless they have already had a reasonable request for a normal interview turned down.

Ideas for programmes

Some PR managers and consultancies are very good at exploiting the power of television – but many have yet to make the most of it. True, TV is hard to get on to because of the relatively small number of programmes compared to the print media. And it does require a degree of sophistication beyond simply sending a release and the brainless follow-up call ('Did you get our press release?').

But a little thought, imagination and persistence can do wonders. Watching programmes can give clues to the criteria for an interesting programme or news item. For a start, something has to be original. It needs to be a new development or something which is being shown for the first time. If the subject is familiar then it requires a new insight into what goes on behind the scenes.

It must be informative. People often like to feel they are being educated and increasing their knowledge of the world about them. It must have good visual content. The viewer wants to see something new, not just hear it. And above all it must be entertaining. The harshest enemies of responsible business presentation on television are the other channels. It only takes the flick of a switch to leave the breathtaking excitement of the moulding shop at the Mickey Mouse Machine Tool Company and change to football or a good western.

Take a building company, for example. The camera crews will not come rushing to the builder's yard to film piles of brick and timber and interview them proudly expounding on their profit figures. But it is another story if on one of the sites they are sinking piles to build houses on what was once useless swamp, or trying out a new building material or a new design. Almost every company has something, somewhere, at some time, which is original and interesting enough to appeal to a television programme.

The next step is to choose the target carefully and approach the right programme for the particular story. Even then it will still be a pretty random process. The most seasoned public relations professionals can never understand why sometimes a great story gets no coverage while the next day a dead mouse under a chair will bring 20 international television crews rushing to the scene. Maybe only one good concept in ten will actually become a television programme or part of one.

Contacts with TV stations and people

Good contacts are important. Cultivating at least one person on each of the relevant programmes has three advantages.

1. Ideas can be bounced off someone who always knows what the programme is looking for.
2. An offering is more credible if the contact is known to them.
3. While never immune from the third degree, tough treatment is less likely without due warning.

Very few television people are as snotty as they are made out to be, and despite the glamour and remoteness of television they are really only journalists underneath – and journalists love new contacts. Breaking the ice should take no more than a phone call. Look up the name of the editor and producer etc in the listings magazines or get a copy of the *Blue Book of British Broadcasting* (Tellex Monitors Ltd). Or ring the switchboard of the production company.

By thinking of a couple of reasons why the programme-makers should be interested in the idea, success is not guaranteed but at least is more likely. These people are professionals and are always looking for new leads.

The editor is the key figure, but will be very busy. The producer is a useful contact, too, but do not overlook the humble researcher. Researchers are the worker ants who go out and do all the delving for the editor or producer. They sift though the newspaper clippings and stories from all sort of sources, looking for material for the next programme.

Businessmen and PR people lavish less attention on them than on editors and producers, yet the programme-makers attach more importance to a story which comes from the researcher (and maybe planted by you) than one which you try to flog direct.

Video news releases

It is also worth considering a VNR (video news release), where a specialist company makes a mini-programme and distributes it to the TV stations (or as syndicated audio tapes to the radio stations) in broadcast quality format. It is the TV equivalent of a press release.

There are mixed views on the efficiency of these. Some VNRs have had spectacular success because they fulfil the various criteria of being colourful, relevant, interesting, etc. Many, if not most, go straight into the plastic recycling bin.

They can also be very expensive, so they require careful discussion and planning with a specialist VNR company – and a healthy whiff of scepticism.

However, since the Greenpeace hijack of news coverage on *Brent Spar*, done by the skilful use of VNRs, many news programmes have declared they will not use them.

18

How: radio interviews

On radio the listener is practically sitting there saying: 'Come on, what have you got to tell me?' In contrast, the television viewer is sitting there like an overfed Roman consul saying: 'Amuse me.'

Radio journalists may slip the old knuckle-dusters on from time to time, but in general radio tends to be more concerned with interesting the listener than with crucifying the interviewee. This can require even more concentration. But at least interviewees usually get a fair hearing on radio.

Local stations are generally run on a shoestring, so with a limited reporting staff they are delighted to have people come to them with material. Is an organisation expanding? Cutting down? Fighting the council over something? Do they have a new product? Are they organising a charity function? Making a profit? A loss? Local radio will take material which a national station would not look at – so long as it is of local interest, and especially if it makes an attention-grabbing noise.

Radio interview techniques

The techniques for radio interviews are basically similar to those for television, but there are a few important differences.

Preparation

The decision on whether to do the interview or not and the information required from the producers is the same as with TV (see Chapter 15). The preparation must be just as painstaking and thorough. Stick to two or three key points, with three or four subpoints for each. Anecdotes are, if anything, even more crucial. A short story, a parable, a brief tale of success or disaster – the radio listener will lap it up.

The same goes for the analogies. The television viewer expects to be shown a picture of something all the time, but the radio listener has to paint his or her own mental pictures.

A good example of creating an image in the listener's mind was the radio presenter who interviewed an expert on hayfever, and looking down a microscope at a speck of pollen, said 'It looks like a tennis ball stuffed with semolina!'

The studio

Radio studios are generally smaller than their television counterparts, and interviewees usually sit at a table with a microphone right in front of them. Surprisingly, a radio studio can be more distracting than a TV one. The lights in a television studio are so bright that people may not be able to see anything, and can concentrate on their message. But in a radio studio the technicians behind the soundproof glass are visible and there are dozens of other distractions.

Someone may drift in to hand a note to the interviewer. Or a face appears behind the glass mouthing 'We're going to the bar – see you there in five minutes.' And it is not unknown in a prolonged programme for the coffee cups to be passed round.

Voice test

Voice tests are conducted for the same reason as on television. Interviewees should speak at the level they intend to use for the rest of the interview. Unlike television, the microphone cannot be ignored.

Manner

It is still a good idea to sit forward in the chair, because it is important to stay wide awake and in command of things. It is even more important to speak clearly and distinctly. On television the viewer is able to do a spot of lip-reading to aid comprehension, but the radio listener can only hear the voice.

It is much easier on radio to refer to notes for guidance. But do not read from them or rustle the paper.

Sincerity, enthusiasm

This is where radio starts to get difficult. In front of a camera there are two ways of demonstrating enthusiasm and sincerity – facial expressions and tone of voice. But the microphone only picks up the latter, so this has to convey everything. The listener has not heard your voice before, so the speaker should sound interested. Vary the pitch and speed.

Listening to the radio will give clues to why some interviewers succeed and others do not. Good radio interviewers are as good at their job as any television interviewer, and will keep things moving, giving the interviewee only 15 to 20 seconds at a time to say their bit. Some, though, simply do not have the knack of keeping an interview alive.

Types of interview

The interview types are pretty much the same as television, but some special handling is required for some of them:

Face to face

Where interviewee and the interviewer do their stuff in the same studio.

Panel

Groups of experts, or people who disagree with one another, come over well on radio. The trouble is that it is harder to get attention. There is no director to turn the camera on a speaker, so participants have to speak out at the right moment and be that little bit more forceful.

Down-the-line

This can be hell. It is bad enough in a TV studio, but at least there is a camera and a monitor to look at. In a down-the-line radio interview the interviewee sits there in solitary confinement, totally remote from the interviewer and any other participants. Remember the tip from Chapter 17 about pretending to be on the phone.

Telephone

The telephone gives radio producers an easy means of interviewing all sorts of people at short notice, at any time of day, and in any location. It is also a popular way of obtaining the view of the general public on phone-in programmes.

Used properly, the telephone can provide a good avenue to get the information across. All that is required is some preparation beforehand and the right kind of handling.

At home or at the office, the speaker can choose how to sit and which room to use. They are on their own territory, which is a psychological advantage. As with any interview outside the studio, avoiding interruptions is important. If in the office, incoming calls should go to someone else. At home, lock the doors. A busy road or other noise source should be out of earshot. It is essential not to listen to the interview on the radio at the same time as this can cause feedback howl.

Conclusion

Used correctly, the media is an invaluable tool for the public relations practitioner. The professional should be aware of how the development of the media has affected its willingness and ability to cover issues. The fast pace of technological change means it is imperative to keep up with the new media and understand how to use them. Indeed, many believe that in the future all contact will be via electronic means such as e-mail and the Internet, rendering the need for printed media obsolete. The increasing range of broadcast media may mean that, while getting on to television may become easier as the number of outlets increases, effective presentation and targeting will become more important to reach the relevant public.

This book is only the beginning for the professional. Background and techniques can only have limited use in a book. What is needed is for the serious public relations practitioner to get out there and do it, and add their own opinions and techniques to those set out here. Above all it should be remembered that public relations and the media have to work together – each would be the poorer without the other. Together, they can produce interesting and informative material, mutually beneficial to both the client or employer organisation and the newspaper or broadcast.

It is hoped that this book has provided some useful information in continuing to improve that relationship.

Bibliography

Books and pamphlets

BBC, *Extending Choice*, BBC, 1992

Belsey and Chadwick (eds), *Ethical Issues in Journalism and the Media*, 1992

Cunningham, J, *Cable TV*, Howard Sans and Co, 1976

Curran, J and Seaton, J, *Power Without Responsibility – The Press and Broadcasting in Britain*, 4th edn, Routledge 1994

Greenwood, W and Welsh, T, *McNae's Essential Law for Journalists*, 12th edn, Butterworths, 1992

IPR, *Public Relations and the Law*, IPR, 1994

Jenkins, S, *Newspapers: The Power and the Money*, Faber and Faber, 1979

Smith, A, *Subsidies and the Press in Europe*, PEP, 1977

Snoddy, R, *The Good, the Bad and the Unacceptable*, Faber and Faber, 1992

Thomas, R, *Broadcasting and Democracy in France*, Bradford University Press, 1976

Williams, A, *Broadcasting and Democracy in West Germany*, Bradford University Press, 1976

Williams, G, *Britain's Media – How They are Related*, CPBF, 1994

Broadcasts

BBC 2, *Money Programme* (Rupert Murdoch), 21 May 1995

   Close up North (Gold Diggers) 23 March 1995

Channel 4, *Satellite Wars*, 26 March 1995, 2 April 1995, 9 April 1995

   Daily Planet, 19 March 1995

   Whole World in His Hands, March 1995

   Naked News, 23 March 1995

Articles

Anglesey, Lady, 'Watchdog firmly on a Legislative Leash', *Guardian*, 4 November 1995

Arden, Z, 'Open Road', *PR Week*, 17 March 1995

Downey, G, 'Press Regulation', *Independent*, 16 November 1992

Fitzwalter, R, 'Tales wag the Watchdog', *Guardian*, 14 October 1991

Fountain, N, 'A Splash of Colour', *Guardian*, 5 December 1994

Gray, R, 'Murdoch Outflanked', *PR Week*, 2 June 1995

Katz, J, 'Tomorrow's Word', *Guardian*, 24 April 1995

Mullin, C, 'Regulations to Save the Nation', *Journalist*, February/March 1995

Murdoch, R, 'Cross? You Bet!', *Guardian*, 29 May 1995

Stott, R, 'Naked Power', *Guardian*, 11 January 1993

Sweeting, A, 'Rolling on and on', *Guardian*, 5 December 1994

Index